MW00856596

FOREWORD *by* ANDREW YOUNG

IT AIN'T BUT ONE!

MY EXTRAORDINARY
LIFE STORY

JASPER W. WILLIAMS JR.

It Ain't But One: My Extraordinary Life Story

by Jasper W. Williams Jr.

ISBN: 978-1-943294-92-3

cover design: Martijn van Tilborgh
cover photo: Jessie Hegland

About Jasper W. Williams Jr.

"Jasper Williams is the prince of preachers. He is a renowned biblical orator, the father of the faithful, and a jewel in the sparkling tradition of the black church."

Rev. Ben Stellmacher

"He is rare, and I am thankful that the African American ministry has such a man as him. Rev. Jasper Williams is one of the most influential men in this city when it comes to religious and church life. And he has been for quite some time."

Dr. C. T. Vivian – Presidential Medal of Freedom Honoree and former President, Southern Christian Leadership Conference

"Jasper is at or near the top when you rank Atlanta's prominent black preachers. He's a teacher and a motivator who penetrates people's souls. He is certainly one of the premier gospel and spiritual innovators in the city."

C.T. Martin - Former Dean of the Atlanta City Council

Dedication

THIS BOOK IS dedicated to the memory of my father, Rev. Jasper W. Williams Sr. (1902-1981).

Proverbs 23:24 states, "The father of the righteous will greatly rejoice, and he who begets a wise child will delight in him."

Daddy, you were more than just a father to me. You were my spiritual guide, my tutor, my role model, my mentor, my friend, my confidant, my leader, and my ultimate example of a man.

It gave me great joy to follow you, as you followed God. When I squandered my talents in misdeeds, and failed to heed your advice, your spirit was there in the depths of my soul. Even as you found your place in the presence of God, your spirit never left me. You will forever be in my heart.

Daddy, it is my hope that one day you can say, "Well done, my faithful son, I am well pleased."

And to every person who has entered my life, whether it was for a season, a reason, or a lifetime: Your impact, great or small, was more than you will ever know. I also dedicate this book to you, for who you are, and who you have helped me to become.

"The Lord bless you and keep you; the Lord make His face shine upon you, and be gracious unto you; the Lord lift up His countenance upon you, and give you Peace."

– Numbers 6:24-26

Contents

Foreword

Rev. Jasper Williams Jr., one of the young giants of the gospel growing out of Morehouse College and the Civil Rights Movement of Dr. Martin Luther King Jr., has enriched the spirit of Atlanta through a creative pastorate and preaching ministry.

After Dr. King's assassination, Jasper and other young preachers developed the tradition of the social gospel and merged it into Atlanta politics.

These young preachers helped me to emerge as a Congressman from the Fifth Congressional District of Georgia, in 1972, and Maynard Jackson as Atlanta's first African-American mayor, in 1973. Neither of us had money for television or mass media, but following Dr. King's leadership, we were embraced by a new generation of young preachers who brought the passion of their preaching and the education of the seminaries and universities into the arena of political action.

On my election day in November 1972, in the midst of pouring-down rain, all night and day, and a landslide national victory for Richard Nixon, the churches, colleges, and a new political awakening produced a 74 percent turn-out of Black voters for my election victory. That was followed by an equally strong campaign for Maynard Jackson's election as mayor, the following year.

Since the victories in the seventies, leaders like Jasper Williams and a network of churches coordinated under his leadership have continued to be the energy and national consciousness of Atlanta, Georgia, and national politics.

In a speech in 1967, Dr. King stated that "10 strong preachers of the gospel are more powerful for good than political parties or trade unions."

Jasper Williams has continued that tradition, not in a self-righteous manner, but by filling the city with a ministry of grace, mercy, and forgiveness.

Atlanta's success is strongly influenced by its ministries and the power of the Spirit which Pastor Jasper Williams so brilliantly preaches, teaches, and organizes throughout the community. He has been and continues to be a blessing through a perpetual, creative, and Spirit-filled ministry.

I am proud to know him as a friend, leader, and brother.

Ambassador Andrew Young
Former Mayor of Atlanta
January, 2019

Acknowledgments

FIRST OF ALL, I am eternally grateful to God for His grace and His mercy toward me. If it had not been for the Lord on my side, I don't know where I would be now. I am who I am because of the calling God placed on my life to preach His Word.

I am thankful for the deacons and members of Salem Bible Church who have gone on to be with the Lord, who saw a glimmer of hope in a young boy from Memphis, Tennessee, and first gave me the privilege of pastoring their church—now for over fifty-five years.

There is no greater love than the love I have for the members of Salem who are currently still with us, serving in various capacities and steadfastly building the kingdom of God. I have endless gratitude for your support of the church and how you have actively worked to provide me with the protected spirituality I have needed to do God's will.

I can never say "thank you" enough to those with whom I have had the pleasure to labor on this gospel journey. There are numerous preachers, pastors, teachers, and lay leaders who have been my mentors and my spiritual eyes and ears.

Many have been patient with me, and have been shoulders to lean on, during my weakest hour. I extend to you my love.

No one in this life could possibly be more important to me in the pursuit of living a godly life than my family. I would like to honor my deceased parents, Rev. Jasper W. Williams Sr. and Alice Williams, whose love and guidance are with me continuously. They were the molders and shapers of my dreams and aspirations. Most importantly, I want to say "thank you" to the mother of my two sons, Rev. Joseph L. Williams, PhD and Jasper W. Williams III. The boys we share provide me with unending inspirations and are among my greatest gifts.

To my dearly beloved sisters, Nealey and Janice, thank you for your love, support, and encouragement. My life would be void without the two of you on my side. To my brother, Apostle Alton R. Williams, thank you for being my partner in ministry as you unselfishly shared all that God gave to you.

A special appreciation to Rev. Zachary Lee, my prayer partner and keeper of my deepest thoughts; you have stood with me and stood for me. Mere words could never describe the value you have added to my life.

There are many, many others, too numerous to name. So to each of you, and those that are getting to know me through this book, I want to say, "I love you," and pray that the peace of God may rest upon you.

I am grateful to Andy Butcher for his collaboration in telling my story, and to Beverly Rice for her assistance with the writing and editing of this book.

Shalom!

Introduction

ANY OF US have a long list of people we can hardly wait to see when we get to heaven. Of course, we all want to see Jesus, but my father, Rev. Jasper W. Williams Sr., is most assuredly next at the top of my list.

So much of who I am as a man is because of the man my father was in years past. I am, without a doubt, the seed of my father. As the saying goes, "The acorn does not fall far from the tree." My constant prayer is that I have made my father proud and that he will utter those words to me, when we reunite.

Through the years, I have been widely honored for the preaching gift God has bestowed upon me; Daddy King, the father of Dr. Martin Luther King Jr., would so often say of me, "It ain't but one!" But it is not the praise of the many that has been my inspiration so much as my undying love and respect for one man: my father. I can truly say that I am my father's son: Jasper W. Williams Jr.

Over the years, while studying the Bible, I have found the prophet Moses to be one of the most intriguing leaders used by God. Moses was a great man of God, with whom I dare not consider myself of equal standing, but it would give me unspeakable joy to engage with him about our respective journeys on earth.

There is no significant comparison between us, other than our call to lead the people of God. While Moses led the Israelites through the wilderness for forty years, I have led a group of "Salemites" for over half a century. And we, too, have been through the wilderness.

Yes, it has been my privilege to serve as pastor of Salem Bible Church in Atlanta for fifty-five years, as I write. There are those who suggest that this unusual length of pastoring should be duly rewarded, whereas I believe that if honor is to be given, it should be rightly given to the congregation that has stayed with the pastor all of those many years.

Though I politely demur, I have often heard people speak of how my life has shadowed the life of Moses in many ways, for he was "no ordinary child" (Acts 7:20, NIV) and my early life as a celebrity child preacher was certainly out of the "ordinary." Just as Moses was raised as a "prince" to inherit Pharaoh's throne, I was raised as a "prince" to inherit my father's pulpit.

For each of us there is also a season of trials, tribulations, and testing. Again, like Moses, I allowed uncontrolled passions to dictate my emotions and actions. I have never murdered anyone, as he did, but I have certainly wounded a few... myself included. Both Moses and I endured some wilderness years as a result of our lack of restraint. Yet, we learned lessons in those difficult times that equipped us to come back as better leaders— stronger, wiser, and humbler.

Before God called Moses home at the age of 120, he was still impactful. According to Deuteronomy 34:7, "His eyes were not dim nor his natural vigor diminished." I cannot say the same concerning myself, even though I contend that, in my mid-seventies, my racquetball game is unmatched by anyone close in age. I am, however, a bit slower on the court these days, so I have learned to use my brain more than my body.

Each time I step into the pulpit, I continue to preach as though my life depends on it. However, my body does not bounce back quite as quickly. I have come to realize after almost seven decades of preaching that my days of bringing God's Word to His people as often as I have done so, are coming to an end.

Please do not misunderstand what I am saying. I am not anticipating imminent death. Indeed, there are dreams and visions that God has given me to impart and implant before my life on earth is done. But as my time of directly leading God's people draws nigh, I feel compelled, like Moses, to pass on whatever wisdom I may have gleaned through the years.

The closing chapters of Deuteronomy record the final words of Moses to the Israelites, while one of the final verses of that phenomenal book recounts how he laid hands on Joshua, his successor, imparting "the spirit of wisdom" (Deut. 34:9).

In telling this story of my life, I hope to impart to future generations, especially young pastors and leaders, what I have learned, in order to equip them for the next level of ministry. I trust that by being candid concerning my missteps, I may be able to help others avoid unnecessary pain and sorrow.

My life has been an adventurous journey, with bumps and hills, and mountains and valleys along the way. When I arrived at what was formerly known as Salem Missionary Baptist Church in Atlanta, in November 1963, the small congregation was meeting in a church building and owned two small houses on each side. At that time the total assets were less than $200,000. Today, Salem Bible Church, as it has become, has two large campuses, owns four assisted living communities, and provides a wide range of ministries to serve those in need. The total assets of Salem Bible Church are more than $65 million. In spite of all of my shortcomings, we have experienced enormous growth, and I believe that this is an indication that God's hand has been on this ministry.

Out of all that we have done at Salem Bible Church, what is really of utmost importance is the many lives that have been changed, through the preaching and teaching of God's Word. Not only have thousands of people made Salem their church home through the years, but I have had the privilege of ministering to hundreds of thousands more, as I traveled throughout the United States, and reached even more through my CD and DVD recordings, in addition to television and radio broadcasts. In my lifetime I will never envision the full impact of my ministry, which gives me a glorious expectation of heaven.

So as I look to what lies ahead for those who will come after me, as Moses did, I feel that it is imperative to pass on words that are both comforting and challenging. Moses spoke to the people on the plains of Moab, in sight of Mount Nebo. I share my heart from my home in Atlanta, from the fortieth-floor window, peeping at a view of Stone Mountain.

I don't believe that Moses would mind if I borrowed a few words from his final address for an exhortation as you read. Never forget, wherever God leads you and whatever comes your way, that:

> *"The eternal God is your refuge, and underneath are the everlasting arms"* (Deut. 33:27).

Jasper W. Williams Jr.
Atlanta
November 2018

CHAPTER ONE

IN MY FATHER'S FOOTSTEPS

A T THE AGE of of seven, I preached my first sermon. It was on Sunday, August 13, 1950, and I spoke about Jesus being "The Living Waters." The moment was exhilarating. It was then that I knew that this "calling" would be for a lifetime. The church gave me eight dollars and thirty-two cents.

That honorarium was four times greater than the average hourly wage during that period, which was quite impressive for a kid—especially a black kid growing up in the segregated South.

While it is true that being paid to preach was exciting, the most indelible imprint was the realization that I could be the man my Daddy had repeatedly told me I would be when I grew up... just like him!

Jasper W. Williams Sr. towered over me, but he also stood tall in the community. During a time when ministers were greatly esteemed and well respected by everyone, my father's prominence gave him an even higher standing among other pastors. Lane Avenue Baptist Church, founded by my father, was considered one of the finest jewels in the crown of churches in Memphis, Tennessee, a city widely viewed as a somewhat modern-day Jerusalem and seen by many as the pinnacle of ministry.

My father had grown Lane Avenue through his God-given gifting of charisma, creativity, and courage. He had a fortitude of spirituality and practicality which has been a conviction within my life—that, yes, our Great God can perform miracles, but He also requires commitment and dedication from those whom He has anointed to do His will.

My father was born in Rankin County, Mississippi, to Henry Williams, a Methodist preacher. When my father was two years old, his daddy died. His mother raised him, his brother, Alton R. Williams, and two sisters in the Baptist tradition in which she grew up. It was through both their father's legacy and their mother's Christian values that the bloodline flowed: both boys would become preachers.

Like many of us, my father had to overcome many challenges as a young preacher. He married his first wife after she became pregnant, and worked hard to provide for his new family, which included selling chickens. As most men, my dad wanted to be honorable as the father of his first child; however, the marriage did not last, and within a few years the stormy relationship ended in divorce.

The fact that God doesn't write people off when they make mistakes was evident in my father's life. He was steadfast in what God had called him to do. Just as he was resolute in his calling, he knew that a wife was essential to his ministry; therefore, Daddy began to seek God's guidance for someone suitable. It was during this time that his best friend, Walker, suggested that he knew just the "right lady."

As God would have it, Walker was right: Alice Stewart was from Greenwood, Mississippi, in the Delta. Daddy would often smile as he shared the story of their first kiss. After dating for a while, he said, they finally locked lips, and it was the "sweetest kiss I ever had in my life."

My parents married and lived in Clarksdale, Mississippi, where my father began pastoring full-time. He pastored four churches and would rotate to a different church each Sunday. Ministry was both demanding and rewarding; nevertheless, his aspirations were larger than pastoring in a small county.

In addition to being the birthplace of the Blues and the home of great barbecue, Memphis was also a religious epicenter. It was the place every preacher desired to find a pulpit. If a preacher pastored in Memphis, he had "arrived." The notable Rev. C. L. Franklin, the "man with the million-dollar voice," was among the young preachers who first became well-known there.

Daddy's opportunity to pastor in Memphis came when the pulpit of St. Mathis Missionary Baptist Church was vacated. The church leaders invited him to preach and were enthralled with what they heard, quickly offering him the position of pastor. Daddy's preaching and personality enabled the church to grow, and it wasn't long before he was asked to become the pastor of a larger church in the city, Columbus Baptist Church.

I was the first of my parents' four children. I was born on July 22, 1943, while Dad was pastoring at Columbus Baptist. Before my second birthday, he was on the move again—this time would be the last. He left Columbus Baptist with a handful of people who wanted to be a part of where God was leading him, and started his own church.

Lane Avenue Baptist Church had a very modest beginning. Its name came from the street where it was located, in a house that my dad had purchased and converted. Its footprint would enlarge significantly within the next thirty years under the strong leadership of my father, becoming one of the premier churches in the city. In the midst of Lane Avenue's now-extensive campus, the original building still stands.

It was Lane Avenue where I made my public proclamation of faith, where I preached my first sermon, and where I learned so much about people, preaching, and pastoring, all while watching my father at the helm.

In the years since its beginning, my ministry has taken me literally to hundreds of churches across the country to minister personally, and to many more on radio, television, and through live recordings. Yet it was Lane Avenue in Memphis where the seeds of my ministry were planted, watered, and began to increase.

•••

THE GROWTH OF Lane Avenue Baptist Church was due in part to Daddy's innovative ideas. His passionate preaching was certainly an inspiration to many, but he realized that he needed to harness something more, and that led him to the technology of that day—radio. With radio, his range of ministry could extend much further. Daddy started a radio broadcast every Sunday afternoon on a local station, WDIA, the first in the country programmed entirely for African Americans.

Daddy purposely scheduled the broadcast for Sunday afternoon because church services were held in the morning and evening, which meant that people could listen to him between services. The radio audience grew, and then God did something incredible; even my dad exclaimed this was unforeseen. Within a few years, WDIA switched from five thousand watts to fifty thousand watts, which allowed broadcasts to go beyond the city limits. Daddy's preaching could now be heard throughout Tennessee, Arkansas, Mississippi, and parts of Alabama, Louisiana, and Missouri. It was estimated that WDIA reached a tenth of America's black population.

I often refer to this occurrence as an important lesson for leaders: Praying and planning are important, but preparation comes with God's timing. You must always be ready to seize the moment when it presents itself.

I remember a woman telling how she had walked down a street in Memphis and heard Daddy preaching all along the way, saying each house she passed was tuned into his program on WDIA. As his name and fame spread throughout the mid-South, people came in throngs to hear him preach in person.

With a thriving church that kept him extraordinarily busy, Daddy could have never imagined what God had in store for him. Yet he never lost focus on the future he believed God had in store for me.

After learning of my mom's first pregnancy, Daddy excitedly said that God told him that the baby would be a boy and that he would become a "great preacher," "a world's wonder" who would go a long way in ministry. This wasn't just a proud prospective father's boast; he truly believed God had spoken to him, and he spoke it to me and over me, time and time again.

"When you get older, you're going to become more like me," he would say. "You're going to get closer to God."

Daddy may have been certain about what he spoke, but it wasn't something he tried to make happen. Perhaps he had the WDIA experience in mind. He seemed content in knowing that things would happen in God's perfect timing.

• • •

IT IS NOT unusual for children to grow up mimicking their environment, so it should not be a surprise that I would emulate a preacher as a small boy. I would retell Bible stories I knew to everyone who would listen. If one of our chickens died, I would preach the funeral in the backyard. My sisters' dolls were regularly baptized by me.

Daddy may have spoken the vision over my life, but it was only when I told him I was ready to preach, at six years old, that he responded. I didn't sit on the "mourner's bench," which was the church's custom when someone wanted to give their life to Jesus. Without celestial fireworks or heavenly choir, one Sunday I got up from my seat in the balcony, walked down to the front of the church and told Daddy I was ready to join church and follow Jesus.

The following week, I was baptized. It was only a few days later that I went to Daddy again and told him that the Lord had called me to preach. Given that Daddy had been telling me for as long as I could remember that I would be a preacher, I thought he would be excited. Instead, the non-committal response he gave me was rather surprising.

"Okay," he said. "I hear you, but I have a couple of questions to ask."

"Yes, Daddy," I said. "Ask me whatever you want."

"If God has called you to preach, what are you going to do with the toy guns you play cowboys with? Preachers aren't supposed to carry guns," he stated.

"I am going to give them away," I said without a thought. "I will never play with them again."

Daddy nodded his head in approval. Then he asked, "What will happen if you go to preach for someone and they don't pay you any money?"

I answered, "Daddy, I'm not preaching for money, I am preaching because God has called me to preach." With that response, he seemed thoroughly satisfied.

Daddy was always a man who stood on his convictions, and he exemplified that steadfastness when he determined I was ready to walk in what he had spoken over my life for years. Some people did not believe a young boy should be allowed to preach, maybe thinking that a child would not have anything meaningful to say.

Perhaps they had not read Matthew 21:15-16, where "they were indignant and said to Him, 'Do You hear what these are saying?' And Jesus said to them, 'Yes. Have you never read, Out of the mouth of babes and nursing infants You have perfected praise.'" Or maybe they felt it was too much pressure to place on such small shoulders.

There were many critics, but Daddy simply ignored them. He laid the foundation for my preaching by grooming me on how to speak, what to speak, and rehearsing with me over and over again. Soon after my seventh birthday, my parents bought me a new suit for my first sermon. Daddy called a special evening service that drew a "packed house." I am sure many were there out of sheer curiosity.

I will always remember standing on a stack of Coca-Cola crates so I could be seen over the podium. Preaching as a child was both frightening and exciting. However, there was nothing else that I wanted to do. While most boys dreamed of becoming a professional athlete or a pilot, I had dreams of preaching, just like Daddy.

Each time I preached a sermon, he would critique the message, with constructive feedback on my strengths and weaknesses. There was always room for improvement.

The pulpit at Lane Avenue was always warm and welcoming, which provided me an opportunity to perfect my preaching. WDIA brought in numerous speaking engagements from all over for Daddy, and many times he would take me with him as he traveled to preach. Not only did this allow me to hear him and learn from him, I was also given a chance to preach to those I did not know.

I vividly remember one particular occasion, when he took me with him to Dyersburg, Tennessee, to preach a revival. The pastor greeted my father, and asked who I was.

"This is my son," Daddy told him.

"I see," the pastor said. "Why did you bring him with you?"

"He's a preacher," Daddy replied. "He's going to preach one night, and I will preach one night."

"We didn't invite you to bring your son," the pastor stated. "We wanted you."

"Well," my father said, "if you don't want my son, you don't want me. We will leave, now."

The pastor's heart changed immediately, and I was allowed to preach.

Wherever we went together, Daddy and I would alternate preaching. Whether I was good or bad, they only got what I preached to them that evening.

It was only a matter of time before the word of my preaching began to spread. I became in the eyes of many churchgoers a "celebrity." Some would point at me and say, "Look, there is that boy preacher everyone is talking about."

Being a preacher was not the only aspect that set me apart from my peers while growing up. As a family we enjoyed a comfortable status and a level of income beyond most in the black community. We were not exactly rich, but Daddy's success meant that we were, by comparison, well-to-do.

To generate additional income, I had a photograph of me along with my dad, which was available when we traveled. I was pictured in a sharp suit, under the headline, "I will hide it from the wise and prudent, and reveal it unto babies." I sold each photograph for 25 cents.

• • •

WHATEVER CELEBRITY STATUS I may have had when we traveled, the temptation of getting too puffed up was quickly diminished when I returned home and went to school. Some of the bigger kids would call me names. "Old preacher," they would shout as they passed by, thumping me on my head.

The torment made me certain of my calling and more determined to exceed all expectations. It was never a thought to retaliate in anger. What could have very easily been a setback was instead a "setup" and gave me strength. The baiting was like a furnace that heated and purified the raw ore I'd inherited from Daddy.

He demonstrated a singular drive to achieve a goal regardless of the obstacles. Although my dad's natural gifting had earned him a reputation as one of the best preachers around, he was concerned that some might dismiss him because he had no formal education. He did not want to be known as just a good "whooper," or a preacher with style and passion but no real substance; he wanted to be educated.

Daddy studied at both Howe Institute in Memphis and the American Baptist Theological Seminary in Nashville. He soon discovered that neither of these schools offered the certification he was looking for. Researching further, he learned he needed basic qualifications for admission to the school of his choice. He enrolled in Booker T. Washington night school for two years, and soon earned his high school diploma.

Daddy continued to pursue his education, attending S.A. Owens Junior College for two years, and Rust College in Holly Springs, Mississippi. For two years, he drove each morning to Mississippi, until he graduated with a B. A. Degree. Meanwhile, his church continued to prosper and he continued to travel, preaching revivals.

Education began to captivate Daddy. He later enrolled in Memphis Theological Seminary part-time. Six years later, he became the school's first black preacher to earn a Masters in Theology.

The tenacity of my father fueled my aspirations to run for president of the student council at Melrose High School in Memphis. There were other boys in my class who were qualified academically and also wanted to run for the position. It was a close race.

I placed posters around the school, asking students for their vote. Supporters of my opponents poked out the eyes, nose, and mouth of my pictures. Instead of getting angry, I took advantage of this attack. When it was time to deliver my campaign speech, I addressed the student body, pointing out the way my campaign posters had been defaced.

"You see what my opponents have done to me," I said. "They gouged out my eyes, knocked out my nose, and took out my mouth. I would have never done that. Instead, I went home each night after seeing my pictures on the wall and got down on my knees. I prayed, 'Father, forgive them, for they know not what they do.' We are going to the polls and you are going to vote for student council president of Melrose High School. Just remember this when you go in to vote: If you want someone who's acquainted with the Master, vote for Jasper."

My words brought everyone to their feet, including the teachers. The principal told me later that he had never heard a student give a speech like that, and if I continued in the way in which I was going, I'd truly become a great speaker one day.

His words were encouraging, but even better was winning the election. It was confirmation that an unwavering spirit and the right words will inspire people's confidence and commitment.

CHAPTER TWO

CAUGHT IN THE SHADOW

EVEN THE BRIGHTEST light can cast a shadow, which was often true with Daddy. His passion and drive could be overwhelming, while his admirable single-mindedness could become unyielding to the point of stubbornness. Daddy loved people, but he felt as though he knew what was best for them, and he didn't appreciate being questioned. For him, the situation was either "black or white," there was no shade of gray.

Daddy was unapproachable, and his standards were high. He would not let anyone get by with what he considered to be wrong, but he never held grudges. If a person admitted they were wrong and apologized, he would forgive them and let it go. However, if you were persistent in your wrongdoing, you would more than likely experience his wrath.

As a well-known leader in the community, it was important to him that our family represented him favorably. When friends came to our house to play, Daddy wanted to know things about their family, including where they attended church. My best friend in elementary school was a boy who lived nearby. We loved to play ball and enjoyed spending time together. His mom had a reputation as the community drunk, however, and of course Dad forbid me to continue playing with him.

I didn't see Daddy's tendency for being domineering in my younger years. I held him in high esteem, eager to earn his approval. I loved traveling with him, and sitting in on the many meetings while he conducted the business of the church. I saw, first-hand, leadership in action long before I studied it in school.

I remember once sitting in a meeting with Daddy when something outside the window caught his attention. One of the members of the church was beating his wife on the church grounds. Daddy ran out the door in a flash.

"You can't do that, Brother," he told the man firmly. "God will not permit me to allow you to do that." The man lowered his hand, as Daddy continued to talk to him, and tears started rolling down the man's face, to his chest.

This incident was just one of the interesting things about Daddy. He could be both tough and tender. Even though he set the rules in the home, it was my mother who enforced them with discipline. Yet I was actually more fearful of my dad's look of disapproval than I was of my mother's whippings.

Melrose High School was very close to our home, therefore I would wait to the last minute to get ready for school every morning. Clearly audible from our home, the first bell rang at 7:50 a.m. For me, it was my snooze button, giving me a few extra minutes in bed. Daddy would usually shout from downstairs for me to get ready, and I would always respond that I was doing so—then I'd turn over and pull the covers up.

Some mornings, I would take my shoes and tap on the floor a few times so that it would sound to those downstairs as though I was up and moving about. One day, to my surprise, Daddy came upstairs and caught me in the act of "fake-walking."

"Uh-uh," he exclaimed, "I've caught you! I've caught you! J.W., you have been pretending that you were getting up; now, I've caught you!"

As you may guess, I never tried it again.

One of the hardest things for a parent is to know at what point they should loose the reins and give their children more freedom. This was certainly a fact in our home. With Daddy's continued coaching and correction, I worked diligently on developing as a preacher.

By the time I was eleven or so, I had graduated from learning and delivering Dad's messages to preparing my own—with consistent feedback from him. I had begun to receive numerous invitations to preach at other churches. I was around thirteen years old when I was asked to preach at Second Mount Zion Baptist Church in Denver, Colorado. It was my first time on a plane and traveling alone as a young person, both of which were very unusual in 1956.

It was also around this time that what had been a closely knit relationship between my father and me began to unravel, as our bond was tested and stretched. What should have been natural and healthy for a growing boy, to pull away and make his own decisions, caused tension between the two of us.

Without a doubt, I wanted to follow in my dad's footsteps and preach the gospel; but I wanted to preach in my own style, at my own pace. This was not enough for Daddy; he wanted to dictate the path that my feet took.

Daddy never wanted me to play sports. I don't know whether he feared I might get injured or he thought it would take my attention away from what really mattered. This prohibition was frustrating for me, though. Not only did I enjoy playing sports,

I had a natural athletic ability. I was exceedingly fast, and had a good arm for throwing and catching a ball. Many times we would race each other in the street, and the other kids would cry out, "We can't outrun that preacher boy!"

I didn't have the courage to challenge Daddy to his face, but I would conspire with Mom behind his back. Without Dad knowing, Mom encouraged me and enabled me to play basketball and football at Melrose High. I could not seriously commit to sports, however, although I liked it, and enjoyed playing the games. Since preaching was my first priority, I could not play on weekends, to the dismay of several coaches.

● ● ●

The little conspiracy between my mother and me revealed to some extent the imbalance of my parents' marriage. Not only did my father have a fairly domineering personality, but my mother was thirteen years younger. The conservative values of the times that played out in the roles of men and women were strictly observed. My mother served as the Minister of Music at Lane Avenue, playing the organ each Sunday, but there was no "equal partnership." She was simply an underling to Dad.

It wasn't until I moved away to attend college that I realized how squashed my mother must have felt all of those years. I once came home to visit, and asked her to let me use her car. I was shocked to find cigarette butts in the ashtray, which was evidence that she had been secretly smoking. Women using tobacco was definitely forbidden, according to Dad.

Years after Daddy passed away, I returned home to find Mom wearing pants. Now, to Daddy, a woman wearing pants would have been scandalous. But for me, it demonstrated how Mom had adjusted her life to accommodate Dad's perception of life. In her quiet manner, she rebelled against him, which could explain why she allowed me to play sports and attend dances that he would not have approved.

There was another factor in our home which, looking back, I deem unhealthy in its own way. Ever since I received my first preaching honorarium, Daddy let me keep the money given to me. He encouraged me to be a wise steward, but never made me give account of how it was spent. Instead of taking his advice with sincerity, I splurged on candy and things of little importance. And I soon learned how I could use money to buy favor.

Daddy kept a watchful eye on the family budget, so I would secretly give Mom money for private and personal spending. In return, she facilitated many of my clandestine activities. It was never acknowledged publicly, but privately it was our secret agreement. In essence, I paid her for her "good deeds."

As I continued to move further away from Daddy, girls became an important issue. As long as I can remember, Daddy had warned me about living a godly life. "Don't drink," he would tell me. "Don't smoke." Those addictions I could understand, but when he said, "Don't have too many women," I didn't want to understand that. With Mom covering for me, I had quietly discovered the delights of dating girls.

Finally, I asked my Dad, "What do you mean when you say, 'Don't have too many women'?"

"J.W.," he replied, "the reason you don't want to have too many women is because nobody will love you."

I still did not understand what he meant by this admonition. If I had only pressed for a little more detail, I may have avoided the heartache I and others experienced along this journey.

• • •

AS IT WAS, Daddy must have had some idea of what I was doing, for he would often tell me, "J.W., don't park my car where it shouldn't be, and get caught doing wrong. Please don't disgrace my name."

I listened but I didn't obey. One night, one of my good friends from high school, Booker T., and I took our girls out in Daddy's car. We parked in a secluded area in a nice part of town. Booker T. and his girlfriend were in the back seat and I shared the front seat with my date.

Love was in the air! Suddenly, a bright light was shining through the windows. The police were doing a routine check to find out why such a nice car was parked where it was. They shined their lights on us and made us continue our act while they watched. Thankfully, our parents never found this out. Years later, I confessed this experience in a sermon to my congregation.

As I grew, so did the tension inside of me. One part of me was fighting to be the preacher Daddy had told me I would be, while another part of me wanted to make my own decisions and go a separate way. It was as though the poles on a magnet had been reversed. The thing that had once drawn me to Daddy was now pushing me away. In the past, the thought of being like Daddy was, *Yes, oh, yes!* But then it increasingly became, *There is NO way, I will be like you.*

In drawing away, I made some room for the influence of others. Someone who became an important person in my development as a preacher was Rev. W.M. Fields Jr. , the pastor of Valentine Baptist Church in Memphis. Following the death of his father, he became the pastor of Eastern Star Missionary Baptist Church, where he served for many years.

Several of us younger preachers would visit "Junior," as we called him, on a Saturday to seek his input for our sermons for Sunday. We would tell him what we planned to preach, and he would give us ideas on how to develop the message. He had a special gift for taking a subject and being able to both tie it to Scripture and also make it applicable to life. I would always come away with a list of notes for improving my upcoming sermon. Sitting at his feet made me appreciate how helpful it is to consult with others, even when you are a gifted preacher.

I knew God had given me the ability to preach. I had been nurtured and nourished by my father. But there were others

God had placed in my life, and I increasingly realized I could learn from them, too.

One such person was Rev. E.L. McKinney, who I met through my father. Before he was ordained, Rev. McKinney was known to everyone as "Preacher." People could see the anointing on his life when he led songs in a gospel quartet called The Southern Wonders. Eventually, he acknowledged his calling to the ministry and came to my father for advice and counsel. Daddy took him under his wings, helping to shape him for years of effective ministry at Pleasant Green Missionary Baptist Church in Memphis.

Rev. McKinney valued my father's counsel greatly. He would call every morning about 6:00 a.m. to talk. I'm not sure how it happened, but when I later moved to Atlanta I was added to his daily call list and we quickly became friends.

When Daddy died in 1981, I inherited the early morning conversations with Rev. McKinney. Though he was at least ten years my senior and we were living in different cities, we became close like brothers. We would talk on the phone for hours, sharing thoughts about preaching and church and events happening in our personal lives. He often expressed his concerns for the welfare of his family. I was his "preaching buddy," which is someone every preacher needs.

Until his death in 2007, there wasn't a sermon I preached that I didn't discuss with him. We would tell each other what we were going to preach, and offer suggestions and ideas to make the sermon more effective.

The older I got, the more Daddy began to talk about his vision for my future. His desire was for me to go to college and return to Lane Avenue to share in his pastorate. The more he talked, the more uncomfortable I felt. I no longer felt as though I was being given the coat of many colors worn by Joseph. The promise of influence and opportunity that I once saw had now become a straitjacket.

I knew I had to leave home to become my own man. The more distance I put between us, the better I would be. I graduated from Melrose High and decided to attend Morehouse College in Atlanta—six hundred miles away. Morehouse was the alma mater of Dr. Martin Luther King Jr., whose civil rights campaigning Daddy admired; therefore he held the school in high esteem.

CHAPTER THREE

A VISION OF MY OWN

I AM PROUDLY a tri-state black man from the South. I am a Mississippian by heredity, a Tennessean by birth, and a Georgian by adoption. The final thread of my identity was woven into being when I arrived at Morehouse College in the fall of 1961.

During this particular time, I saw moving to Atlanta as the vehicle by which I would gradually be released from the ties that bound me to Memphis and my father's vision for my life. I didn't realize that Atlanta would actually become my home— the place where I would reside for more than half a century.

Being accepted to Morehouse, one of the nation's premier historical black colleges, was an honor; but honestly, I did not treat it as such. I knew of its revered history, as the fabric from which many African American community leaders had been shaped and refined, including Dr. Martin Luther King Jr. and his father, known to everyone as Daddy King. I also admired and respected the leadership of the Morehouse president, Dr. Benjamin E. Mays, and his great oratorical skills.

Not only did following in the footsteps of such great men seem extremely promising, it also provided the distance I needed to get from under Daddy's dominance, and would hopefully give me a key to unlock the door I was interested in opening—pastoring a church of my own.

When I arrived in Atlanta, a seventeen-year-old with a big dream, I was delighted to discover that the city was a place of great opportunity. Memphis may have had its reputation as the showcase for preaching, but Atlanta was where African American entrepreneurship was flourishing. The prosperity of black-owned businesses was incomparable to any other city in the country: Yates and Milton drugstores, Atlanta Life Insurance, H.J. Russell & Co. construction, and Paschal's restaurant were just a few of the well-known businesses. Without a doubt, I could perceive the rewards of innovation and inspiration.

It wasn't until I got to Morehouse that I discovered I could not major in religion, so I chose sociology as my major and religion my minor. I didn't have an interest in pursuing Sociology as a career, but I heard it was a fairly soft course which didn't require much effort. "If you want easy courses to graduate, sociology is the perfect major," I was told. That suited me, quite well.

Daddy was instrumental in opening doors for me in Atlanta before I even got there. He attended the National Baptist Convention shortly before I left Memphis. At the convention, he met a delegate from Atlanta who introduced himself as Rev. B. Joseph Johnson. He was the pastor at Greater Mount Calvary Baptist Church, and a graduate of Morehouse College.

When Daddy told him that I would be attending Morehouse, he gave my father his phone number and asked that I call him when I arrived. I made contact with Rev. Johnson accordingly. The following Sunday he picked me up in his car and took me to his church. I was very appreciative of his hospitality and sat quietly under his ministry for several months.

I must admit that, even though I was patient, the preacher in me was anxious to come out. One Sunday, Rev. Johnson came to church really sick—he could barely talk. He asked me to assist him by praying over the congregation. As I stood to pray, everything that had been bottled up in me all those Sundays I sat silently came bursting out. I prayed a momentous prayer, stirring the congregation in such a manner that Rev. Johnson actually never preached that morning.

After that prayer, many people wanted to hear me preach an actual sermon. Rev. Johnson arranged a special Sunday evening service—just like Daddy had done the first time I preached ten years earlier. The evening of the service, Greater Mount Calvary was filled to capacity. The exuberance I felt on the inside from those weeks of not being able to preach exploded.

As a result of the power of God manifested in my life, Rev. Johnson invited me to preach a one-week revival at the church. People came from churches throughout the city. Among them was Rev. Johnson's cousin, Dr. E.H. Dorsey, the pastor of Tabernacle Baptist Church. I was invited there to preach, and before long invitations were coming from all areas of Atlanta— another example of how when God places something in our hearts, although we may not see how it is going to happen, we must be prepared to walk through the doors He opens.

The opportunities that I was afforded to preach continued to weaken my already limited academic focus. I did minimum class work in school, completing very few assignments. As my preaching engagements grew, I registered for classes I knew I wasn't going to attend. While I was excited my ministry engagements were increasing, I was sadly failing classes at Morehouse.

Over time, school was no longer a priority. I moved off campus after my first year of college, and rented a room in an older woman's house; partly because she had a telephone, which made it easier for me to manage the many preaching engagements and invitations I was receiving.

•••

Though God seemed to have His hand on me, it's important to acknowledge that oftentimes it was in spite of anything I was doing. I was pursuing the vision I believed God had given me as a six-year-old, but I didn't always choose the right path; yet, God continued to bless me.

My relationship with my dad continued to be challenging. Daddy was still under the impression that I was going to complete my four years at Morehouse and return to Memphis to minister with him and under him. To avoid openly discussing my true feelings, I allowed him to believe his own desire, and quietly went on my way. I would talk to him about the preaching engagements I was receiving, and sometimes ask his advice, however he thought these discussions were essential in my gaining more experience. For what I felt were justifiable reasons, I did not feel compelled to share my true vision with Daddy.

For years, I'd enjoyed having more money than my peers, because of honorariums I received from preaching. Yet I was a very poor manager of money and I hadn't learned to make wise choices in spending. I spent money quickly and easily. In fact, I got so far behind in rent my first year off campus, as a sophomore, that the landlady eventually told me I had to move.

I packed everything I had into my suitcase and left. I thought I could do better going back to the Morehouse College dorm to ask if I could sleep on a friend's floor for a night or two while I contemplated what to do next. On my way down the street I passed a house where the owner, Miss Holly, called out to me.

"Young man," she said, "what are you doing with that suitcase?"

I told her I had to move from where I had been renting a room, and was on my way to find somewhere to stay.

"Well, do you go to school?" Miss Holly wanted to know.

I told her about Morehouse, which seemed to impress her.

'Well, maybe you'd like to live here in my house?"

I couldn't believe my good fortune; just a few minutes after and a few doors down from a setback, I'd found a solution. I hadn't been homeless for a night and God was there, taking care of me. Miss Holly was one more person in a long succession of "right" people at the "right" time who have helped me along the way.

A few churches where I was invited to preach did not have pastors. Many were looking for a preacher to fill their pulpits in the interim. I thought if I did well, I would perhaps be considered for a full-time position. I was disheartened to find my youthfulness worked against me. As it turned out, church members were willing to hear from a young man of God, but they certainly didn't want to be led by one.

Their attitude was typified by the response I received from one church where, when my name came up in the business meeting as a possible candidate for pastor, an old lady said, "That little boy can preach all right, but he don't have no business having our church. I can't have him as my pastor." As time went by, the same words came back from other places: "Too young," "Too young," "Too young."

Sometime in the spring of 1963, I was contacted by the deacons of Salem Missionary Baptist Church. They wanted to know if I was available to preach at Salem on Easter Sunday. They had heard me preach at a tent revival on Simpson Road at the invitation of Rev. E.F. Robinson, a Methodist minister who had sponsored the interdenominational revival. I had left an indelible impression upon them.

Salem Missionary Baptist Church was in the city's Summerhill district, just south of downtown and close to what would become the new Atlanta Braves stadium. Dating back to the 1890s, the red brick church building on Martin Street wasn't particularly noteworthy, but the folks were welcoming enough when I arrived. As I stepped into the pulpit that morning, something inside me said, *This church is mine.*

Even though it was Easter Sunday, I had selected a message unrelated to the season. I chose what I considered the best sermon I had preached thus far, "The Lord is My Shepherd," taken from the 23rd Psalm. This sermon had always made a big impact when I preached it elsewhere, and this Sunday morning was no exception. Salem really seemed to appreciate my passionate delivery and youthful zeal. I left the church with the confidence that the deacons would invite me back again.

As it was, they inevitably called. I was asked to preach on a regular basis throughout the fall. The church knew I was only nineteen years old; they were interested in calling me as pastor, but just weren't ready to appoint a new one before their annual conference in November, they explained. However, I was now presented with a serious dilemma. Dad's advice had always been to never preach more than three times at a prospective church. "They should know after three sermons whether or not they want to call you to pastor," he explained.

I called Daddy for counsel. He knew I was looking to pastor a church in Atlanta, but thought this was only while I was finishing up my studies at Morehouse.

"You're going to have to make up your own mind about that, J.W.," he said when I told him the situation. "I've always found three times to be enough, but it may not be for this particular situation. You're going to need to pray about it and let the Lord lead you." With prayer and counsel, I made the decision to preach at Salem once a month until their conference.

I had turned twenty by the time one of deacons called me on the first Friday evening in November. "This is Brother

Robinson," he told me. "You were officially elected our pastor tonight and we'll be looking for you in church on the second Sunday."

I told him thank you, and that I would see them then.

• • •

Excited as I was at the opportunity to pastor my first church, I knew there would be challenges because of my age. Despite the fact I had more preaching experience than the average man considerably older than me, I still looked like a fresh-faced kid. People who appreciated me in the pulpit may not have much time for me in the pastor's office.

My sense of caution turned out to be warranted. When I arrived, I was given this directive from the deacons: "Preach. Shut up. Sit down." They wanted me to bring God's word each week, and they would control everything else. That was how their leadership worked, much as it did in many Baptist churches elsewhere.

Nevertheless, this was not what I had in mind, nor what I believed was best for the church. Growing up at Lane Avenue, I had witnessed how my father's strong hand had been instrumental in leading the church to the growth it had experienced. I had also observed that even though Dad was determined, he was wise in his leadership. He preferred to win people over to see his perspective, rather than insist on everything going according to his plans.

My robust spirit immediately wanted to exert itself, but I remembered the words of my father. "You've got to preach your way into their hearts," he said, "and that takes time." So I constrained myself and focused on bringing the best message possible every time I stepped into the pulpit. I hoped that my extreme preparation would help me build relationships of trust and commitment.

What I perceived to be the deacons' protectiveness of the church was, at the time, frustrating. When I look back now, I am a bit more sympathetic, even appreciative, of their conservative attitude. These deacons had been at Salem much longer than I had, and wanted to safeguard their members from a young man who had more enthusiasm than experience, regardless of my years of preaching. Another fact was my singleness, which was very unusual for a pastor. I suspect some of them may have wondered whether, as an eligible bachelor, I would pursue their daughters.

When I accepted the pastorate at Salem, services were held two Sundays a month. The pastor would alternate preaching at another church. The deacons stated that if I was going to be their pastor, it would be a full-time position. The church started me with a salary of $50 a week, and gave me a 1964 navy blue Chevrolet Impala to drive.

One of the first ways I worked my way into the people's hearts was when I honored the former pastor. He was elderly, and his ill-health had forced him to step down. I insisted that the church continue to help him financially. The congregation seemed to really appreciate my unselfish spirit, and esteemed me more highly.

While my father counseled me over and over on being patient, he also warned that the time would come when a pastor has to draw a line in the sand. It is important that the pastor makes it clear that they are called by God above anything and everything else. Well, that time came for me soon after the first year of my pastorate. It was an issue for which I don't even remember the details—which shows just how churches can get distracted by things that don't really matter.

Whatever the problem, I felt the church and I had grown to a point where their responsibility to me should have been greater. I called Daddy and asked for his advice. He heard me out, and said, "Well, you just come on home whenever you get ready, J.W."

When I walked to the pulpit the following Sunday, I mentioned the difficulties we were facing in the church. "You know," I said, "my dad told me I could come on home, so I'm just going to leave." I took a folded piece of paper out of my suit jacket pocket, placed it on the pulpit, stepped down, and started to walk toward the door. Of course that started a major uproar, as you could imagine!

"Don't y'all let that boy go! Don't let him leave us!" yelled Mother Caldwell, one of the older ladies in the church. People began to stand up all around the church. There was quite a commotion that Sunday. Anyhow, I never made it to the exit door. As different members called out, begging me not to quit, I knew I had gotten their attention and there was a renewed atmosphere. I turned around, went back to the pulpit, and picked up the blank piece of paper everyone had thought was my resignation letter.

For me, this act of faith enabled me to see the commitment of the congregation. It also rewarded me with an unexpected bonus. Brother Wilson, one of the deacons, said, "Well, you got the Impala when you came, it's time for us to get you a Cadillac. You can go get whatever you want." In addition, he recommended the church increase my weekly pay to $200—with back pay for time passed. The church voted unanimously in favor of the recommendation.

I grew up watching Daddy manage various issues in the church, and knew that the pastor often found himself caught in the middle of different factions and groups within the congregation. The origin of the conflict may have nothing to do with church per se—it could be jealousy over a romance or some kind of inter-family rivalry—but the pastor would somehow get thrust into the middle of things by those involved who would try to use their relationship with him as a way of manipulation. As a result, I knew a pastor had to be more than just a good preacher; he also had to be a clever politician and a wise diplomat.

I learned that you have to know how to manipulate people—in a positive manner. We often think of manipulation only as a negative thing, and it can be—like the way I used money to buy favor with my mother. But when a doctor manipulates a broken bone, it's positive. He is working to restore it to the way it was intended to be, so healing can come about. In the same way, I learned to read the behavior of people.

CHAPTER FOUR

LEARNING TO LEAD

T HE FIRST BIG challenge I faced at Salem came when I realized we needed to relocate. My anointed preaching had made Salem a household name. We now had the problem of getting the many members inside the church. What made matters worse was that when the Braves played at Atlanta Stadium, there was no parking in the area. I had arranged for us to rent the parking lot of E.P. Johnson Elementary School, which was located across the street, but that soon became too small. The church was growing so rapidly, we simply had to find a new place of worship.

Not surprising to me, many of Salem's long-standing members did not want to leave the present location. They had a lot of history intertwined in the church building. Many of them had been baptized, or married, or had buried loved ones there. For them, it wasn't just a church building, it was sacred ground. Still, I knew that we were not going to grow where we were; therefore, I continued to cast my vision before the church deacons.

The deacons gradually agreed, reluctantly joining my search for a suitable piece of land by 1965. One time they suggested we buy a two-acre site that was selling for about $80,000. I thought the price was high, and we could do better. I enlisted the help of a church member who was in real estate. He came to me with a potential site that was twice the size and half the price. The four-and-a-half acres were about twelve miles away, on the west side of the city, and could be purchased for $44,000.

I went to a black-owned bank and got a loan to be paid back over eight years. Taking that giant step caused the members to be more giving, which allowed us to pay off the total loan within merely eight months. I was overwhelmed with encouragement!

Though we now owned the land, we needed money to develop it. Returning to the bank, I was told they were willing to help, but we had to have "some skin in the game"—we needed to raise $25,000 to show we were serious. With the task of raising this considerable sum before us, we started working. We raffled almost everything imaginable—hogs, cows, old cars, you name it. When the time was right, we reached our target, and now we were able to begin work on the new church located on Baker Road.

All of this took place during the early years of my ministry in which I laid down some crucial financial foundations. It was quite a learning experience for me, given that I had not handled my own money particularly well. I remember when, in my first couple of years at Morehouse, before I was pastoring, I realized I had burned through all the tuition money Daddy had given me.

I called home to ask him whether he would pay my tuition, again.

"Again, J.W.," he said. "Didn't I give it to you once already?"

"Yes," I said, "but I spent it."

"Well, J.W., I guess what you need to do is pack your bags and come on home."

No way was I going to move back home! I told the young lady I was dating, who would later become my wife, of my dilemma. She graciously gave me the money so I could stay in school.

This situation, and Daddy's advice about financial matters involving the church, were on my mind when we embarked on our Salem Missionary Baptist Church building program. Dad had drilled into me that you never, ever, steal money from the church.

It was not uncommon at that time for pastors to award a contract to a particular business with the understanding that the company would give the pastor money under the table as a "thank you." Though I had not been especially careful with my own money, I had never done anything wrong with it, and I was determined that everything would be honest and trustworthy in the church. Sadly, honesty was not always the policy of some church members.

Salem, like many other churches of its caliber, had different auxiliaries responsible for numerous aspects of church ministries, from the choir to the usher board. Each auxiliary collected dues from members of the church and had the responsibility of managing their own money. This strategy, unfortunately, left plenty of room for some of it to be misdirected or even misappropriated.

Once, I discovered that one of the members over the finances was siphoning off large sums of money from the church's accounts. I didn't want to go to the deacons with the information, to have it escalated, so I decided to minimize the damage. I assigned specific people to be in charge of certain categories of the money—one to handle the checks, one to count the notes, and another to handle the currency. The person I was seeking to constrain still managed to sneak out a couple rolls of quarters in his socks, but he eventually got too old and sick for the financial responsibilities, which was a welcome relief. With his departure, the mystery of the financial loss was solved.

This was one of the greater lessons in leadership I was taught by Daddy: "You need to be careful to choose your battles. It's not wise to make everything a hill to die on. Sometimes it's best to be patient and let time and nature take their course—the old guard will in time move away or fade away."

Thankfully, there were some people who really believed in me during this whole process. At one point we had to halt building the new church because we'd run out of money. Visiting the site, I was sitting down on the curb, not knowing what to do, when one of the deacons came by to see me. He dropped a bag down at my feet.

"What is this?" I asked.

"Take a look," he told me. "Take a look."

When I opened the bag, inside was $3,000 in cash.

"'You just take that and let it go as far as it can," he told me. "Give it back to me whenever you're able."

• • •

THOSE KIND OF moments were a great encouragement. Still, the construction and move was not without its problems. In another instance, the bank froze the loan when the rumor mill linked me to a murder!

To this day I don't understand how I was implicated in such a thing. The music minister at another church in Atlanta was killed and somehow word got around that I was responsible. I'd never spoken to the man, but the rumor was enough to scare the bank.

We called a special church meeting to address all the turmoil, and the bank sent one of its senior executives. The church was packed. One of the first to speak was a long-time church member who stood up and said of me, "This boy has done more for this church than anyone, and now they're just trying to destroy him. Everybody who's with our pastor, let's show the bank." With that everyone stood to their feet, and soon after the bank reversed its decision. The loan was reactivated, and the building of the church continued.

In 1970, as time drew near for us to finally relocate to our new home, there was still a cloud of resistance. The director of the choir came to me and said that the members didn't want to move, and if I didn't let her continue in her role as director, she would make sure that the choir didn't support me.

"Well," I told her, "you won't be in charge, and we are going to move."

The following Sunday, I announced that on the first Sunday in March I would be leading a motorcade from Martin Street to our new home on Baker Road.

"Those of you who don't want to go, stay here," I said. "Those of you who want to come with me, we'll be leaving at eight o'clock in the morning."

It was reminiscent of the time I'd faked my resignation a few years earlier, although I was a little nervous in the following days. The next Sunday morning I was thrilled to see a fleet of vehicles ready to proceed when I pulled up on Martin Street. We had a final prayer in the old building, and with me leading the procession in my Cadillac, I felt somewhat like Moses leading the Israelites out of Egypt to the Promised Land.

Unlike the Israelites, we had police assistance—and needed it. The convoy of vehicles stretched for a little over eight miles, making it one of the longest motorcades the city had ever seen. I knew the length of the line because as I turned onto our new property on Baker Road, I heard the police officer directing traffic on the radio with a colleague guiding the back of the line. The police officer told him they were just passing Paschal's, which was located at that time on Hunter Street.

The skies opened up on this glorious day for Salem, and thus it truly "rained on our parade." There was absolutely nothing that could muffle the sense of accomplishment and anxiety I felt when we walked into our new church home. Because the parking lot had not been laid, the cars had imprinted the wet ground, so we were careful to wipe the mud off our shoes. Nobody complained; we were all happy to be in our new church home.

What made the day even more special was my father, the guest preacher, delivering the first sermon in our new church. Dad came down from Memphis for the occasion, bringing two busloads of his congregation to join us in our celebration. He spoke about Nehemiah's rebuilding the walls of Jerusalem.

I was glad Daddy was there to share in the celebration. So much of what I had learned from him had played an integral role in getting Salem to this new place, not just geographically but spiritually and organizationally, as well.

His presence was also an unspoken seal of approval and a sign of his blessing. We never talked directly about it, but by this time Daddy knew Salem was my church home and I would not be returning to Memphis to minister with him. Maybe he saw Salem as an extension of his ministry, through which I had learned to spread my wings and soar.

Daddy also knew I had been embraced by some of Atlanta's most respected church leaders. At first, a few members of the city's ministerial association had been cautious towards me. They were a little leery of this young preacher with the unusual style. Others had been welcoming and affirming—notably Dr. Martin Luther King Sr., or Daddy King as he was known, who my own father respected greatly.

As Dr. Martin Luther King Jr. rose to prominence, only to be tragically extinguished, Daddy King remained a man of great influence in Atlanta and his affirmation of me opened many doors. It was a relationship from which I benefited in many ways.

On one occasion, he and I were driving together when I was stopped by the police. As the white officer approached my car from the rear, he paused to note my tag on the ticket he was writing. Daddy King told me, "Now don't you say anything. Just let old Dad handle this."

When the cop arrived at my window he glanced over in surprise at Daddy King in the passenger's seat.

"Oh, Daddy King," he said.

"Yes," he said. "Just give me the ticket, would you?"

The cop looked a little awkward. "Well, I didn't know you were in the car..."

"No, that's all right," Daddy King said. "Just give me the ticket."

As the officer walked back to his patrol car, Daddy King turned to me. "Now Son, don't worry about this. You just go on driving like you're supposed to drive and take old Dad home where I need to go, and all will be fine."

I never heard any more about the ticket.

It was obvious that Daddy King had a deep affection for me, and it was evident that he had taken me under his wings. He loved my lively preaching, which was very different from his more temperate demeanor. "It ain't but one," he would always say when he saw me. Once he retired from Ebenezer Baptist Church, Daddy King would come to Salem services whenever he got a chance. I always invited him to speak to the congregation, if he wanted to.

"Yeah, let me just speak and say this," he would say. "I want Salem to know this preacher right here, Jasper Williams, 'It ain't but one.' When I'm dead and gone just remember what old Dad said: When you hear preaching like this, it ain't but one."

• • •

ALMOST ALL OF the members from the old location followed the church to Salem's new home on Baker Road. However, soon after moving I realized some members were not support-ive of the vision I had for growing the church. Their opposi-tion was silently demonstrated by their refusal to give money in the offering.

As a result of their resistance the church experienced high-er mortgage notes, higher utility bills, higher construction costs—and less income. I expected the members would be generous and willing to give more than before, since we had managed to pay the first loan back in eight months instead of eight years. As a pastor with a vision, their defiance was ex-tremely disappointing.

In order to transform Salem's long-standing financial tradi-tions, it was important to move the congregation from the old practice of paying dues. I wanted them to know that tithes and offerings were biblical, while paying dues was not scriptural. Paying dues suggests you belong to a club, and bringing tithes and offerings speaks to kingdom living. Encouraging tithing was not just biblical, it was also practical. Consolidating the church's money under my radar was a strategy to reduce the auxiliaries' subtle power structure.

Transitioning from paying dues to paying tithes was a slow process. People are often resistant to change, especially when money and power are involved. I engaged members to encour-age others to tithe by sharing their personal experiences. I'd ask a member of the congregation who had started tithing to share in a service how tithing had blessed their life, thereby motivat-ing and inspiring others to tithe. More and more, people slowly began to embrace the teaching I presented on tithing.

In the meantime, the bills had to be paid. Some people in church leadership think it's unspiritual to talk about money, but Jesus had a lot to say on the subject. A church cannot sur-vive without money. In ministry, there is hardly anything you can do if you're broke! After bringing Salem to its new home, I had to make sure the bills were paid.

Once again, I discovered that when God has given you a vision, you may have obstacles, but the solution is in God's hand: He is the answer to all of our problems.

God had given me the gift of preaching; it was up to me to use it. With a heart to see the needs met at Salem, I began accepting as many external preaching engagements as possible. I would preach on Sunday mornings at Salem, pack my suitcase with books to prepare for the next week's sermon, and head out to a revival in another city, such as Chicago or Detroit. There I would preach every night, Sunday through Friday. During the day, I would spend time studying my sermon for Salem. I would finish the sermon when I returned home on Saturday.

With God's sustaining grace, I was able to keep this rapid pace for at least forty weeks out of a year, for many years. I used the money to pay down the debt at Salem. It was exhausting at times, but as the pastor of Salem there was no other alternative.

My ministry also had such an enormous impact throughout the nation that the rewards were greater than the task. Traveling was often burdensome, but the preaching of the gospel was a joy. Every time I stepped into the pulpit, my passion for preaching became overwhelming. I always had the feeling that God had ordained me for preaching His Word. In addition, it was gratifying to know I was following in my father's footsteps. Dad had ministered throughout the mid-South; now my ministry allowed me to travel to all of the forty-eight contiguous states.

Similar to my dad's experiences, I took advantage of radio to expand my reach. He had broadened his ministry through radio, so one day I went to WAOK Radio in Atlanta to ask if the station had air time available. They offered me a slot for one hour, at 10:00 p.m. on Sunday. In order to have a live broadcast, I started a late-night service. In the beginning people came out for the service, but the attendance soon fizzled. I was not surprised about the drop in attendance, considering the fact that people had to go to work the next morning. I decided to drop the live broadcast and record the morning's service instead.

Being on WAOK Radio benefited Salem and me in many ways. Not only did people hear me preaching and would come and hear me in person, I also developed relationships with some of the disc jockeys at the station. They would promote Salem on the air. "Don't forget to go to Salem Missionary Baptist Church," they'd tell the listeners.

As my reputation as a prolific preacher spread, I saw other opportunities to extend my ministry and help meet Salem's financial needs. One came from the example of Rev. C.L. Franklin who, next to my father, was most instrumental in molding and shaping me into the preacher I am. I often took notes from his ministry book of preaching.

More than anyone in his era, Rev. Franklin had brought a new dimension to preaching that touched and inspired people. Just as black music exploded in the secular world through singers such as James Brown, Rev. Franklin brought that same passion and showmanship from the stage to the pulpit. Choosing colorful, tailored suits over the traditional black suits and white shirts worn by old-time preachers, he made preaching fashionable in so many ways.

Sermonizing and singing in a unique way, his "gospel caravan" events drew huge crowds from across the country. It was on this platform that his daughter, Aretha, who would become one of the best-selling musical artists of all times, made her debut.

Rev. Franklin had been an inspiration to me for a long time. Our families had known each other many years. Dad, his brother Alton—whom I knew as Uncle Buddy—and Rev. Franklin had known each other while living in Mississippi. Their bond strengthened while they were all pastoring in Memphis, though Rev. Franklin would leave Memphis for New York and then Detroit, where he led New Bethel Baptist Church for nearly forty years.

While he was in Memphis, Rev. Franklin developed a close relationship with Uncle Buddy. The two played checkers together every day, and it was through Uncle Buddy's example that I developed my own love for the game that I continue to play to this day.

I did not know Rev. Franklin personally, as I had Rev. Fields and Rev. McKinney, but as a young boy I spent countless hours in my room listening to his recorded sermons over and over again, trying to absorb his style. He could bring a Bible story to life like no one else. When he talked about grapes, you could picture them, plump and shiny, and taste the sweetness in your mouth!

Years later, Rev. Franklin praised me for my skills in the pulpit. For me there was no greater measure of having arrived as a preacher than receiving his stamp of approval.

CHAPTER FIVE

IN THE SPOTLIGHT

KNOWING HOW HIGHLY successful Rev. Franklin's recorded sermons had been, once I arrived at Salem I followed his lead. The first sermon I released was "Clear Shining After Rain," recorded by Atlanta's Church Door Records. I purchased the label from the company and followed with many more recordings of my sermons. The sales generated income to help me support Salem. In addition, new doors for preaching engagements were opened as the name Jasper W. Williams Jr. spread throughout the land.

As time passed, I was given the opportunity to show my appreciation for Rev. Franklin's influence in my life. For at least three years, Rev. Franklin had invited me to preach his annual revival at New Bethel Baptist Church. In 1979, Rev. Franklin was shot during a home invasion, leaving him in a coma. After this tragedy, I continued to preach the annual revival. Each time I preached, I would take a generous offering and give it to Rev. Franklin's family, to help care for him.

When Rev. Franklin passed in 1984, the family discussed who should eulogize their beloved father. The names of several well-known preachers and pastors were considered, such as Rev. Jesse Jackson and Dr. Caesar Clark. Someone spoke and said, "I think we should ask Rev. Jasper Williams."

Remembering how I had quietly helped provide financial care for their father for many years, the family decided together that I should be the one to eulogize Rev. Franklin. This was an incredible honor, and I was humbly grateful to be asked. I contemplated what I could preach to adequately project the legacy of this great man of God. I reflected on a sermon I had preached at Salem recently. It was the dynamics of that sermon which inspired me to preach "A Good Soldier" at Rev. Franklin's over-flowing memorial service in Detroit.

The funeral was attended by a Who's Who of black church pastors, preachers, and community leaders across the country. The passion and power of his preaching was evident by the presence of those he had impacted. For me personally, being extended the privilege of honoring the man who had been so influential in my life and that of countless others was a tremendously moving experience. As I preached, I felt something of the mantle of Rev. Franklin's spirit enter into my soul.

A recording of the message I preached, packaged along with a twelve-page program from the memorial service, became a big seller and opened many more doors of opportunity. If there is one lesson I learned from this experience, it is this: Love and kindness are never wasted. They always make a difference. They bless the ones who receive them, and they bless you, the giver.

When I accepted the call as pastor of Salem I never thought I would own a record company. Having founded Church Door Records primarily as a mechanism for my sermon recordings,

I also used the label as a platform for new music. Among our releases were The Daytonians' *Let Jesus Work It Out*, Norris Turner's *Give God a Chance*, and the Sensational Five Singing Sons' *Hotel Happiness*.

Without a doubt, though, Church Door Records is best known for elevating Dottie Peoples to greater prominence. For this reason alone, I consider purchasing the label a worthy investment.

It was in the mid-sixties when I first heard the voice that would earn Dottie the nickname "Songbird of the South." I was invited to preach at Greater Mount Moriah Baptist Church in Dayton, Ohio. In this church *everyone* could sing—the pastor, the deacons, everyone. But there in the choir was a young girl named Dottie, with the most powerful voice I had ever heard.

As Dottie got older, singing was her career. She earned a living opening for famous performers like Stevie Wonder and The Rolling Stones. Later she became a successful jazz singer. Not long after Dottie moved to Atlanta she became a member of Salem. One Sunday morning, I asked her to sing and she was amazing! She turned the church "inside out and upside down."

Later Dottie assisted Salem's music ministry by directing the choir. There were times when she accompanied me when I traveled. She would sing before I got up to preach. Her debut album on Church Door Records released through Air Records, *God is Able*, paved the way for a ministry in music that continues to touch people even now.

I never considered myself a singer, but Dottie discerned my ability. Musicality had always been a part of my preaching, just as it had been with Daddy and with Rev. Franklin. However, I had never given serious thought to singing. Because of Dottie's encouragement and coaching, I recorded three albums of music that touched people and helped support the financial needs of Salem. Years later I was rated high on the *Billboard* charts for the album *Landmark*, a feat I could have never imagined or achieved without Dottie.

I would not have mentioned how I was asked to deliver the eulogy for Rev. Franklin except for the fact that it emphasizes a principle I have tried to practice throughout my years of ministry: generosity. Over the years I have always been exceedingly generous with money. Where there is a need, I do not hesitate to try to help meet that need.

This is another lesson I learned from my father. He did not make a show about what he did, but he quietly helped out whenever he could. The impact of this was brought home to me unexpectedly one time when I was traveling to preach somewhere. I was in an airport when a man came up to me and asked if I was Jasper Williams Jr.

I told him I was, and he went on to tell me how much my father had meant to him. The man had been planning to drop out of school when he was younger because he could not afford to stay, he said, when Daddy had learned about the situation and stepped in. My daddy had paid for the rest of the man's education.

I tried to continue with that same kind of quiet support. I felt privileged to discreetly press money into Daddy King's hand whenever I saw him. In fact, I had given him money when he came to Salem the morning of his death.

In 1984 and in 1988, Rev. Jesse Jackson ran for president of the United States, which was a great expense and a financial strain. To effectively run for the presidency he had to resign from leading Operation PUSH. I was pleased to be able to ensure that his family was provided for so that he could give himself wholeheartedly to his campaign.

As stated earlier, I am not revealing this to make me out to be someone special, but to highlight how when we take care of people God puts in our path, He will take care of us. I don't believe in giving in order to get something in return; at the same time, there is no denying that when you give to others without expectation of getting back, you often get much more than you give. This really should not be surprising: After all, Jesus did promise in Luke 6:38, "Give, and it will be given unto you: good measure, pressed down, shaken together, and running over will be put into your bosom. For with the same measure that you use, it will be measured back to you." This has certainly been my experience.

Giving to others was one of the ways I found to embody a principle that my father always drilled into me. "J.W.," he would tell me, "keep your hand in God's hand and treat people right."

I have tried to live by this principle, although with varying degrees of success. Each week I encourage the congregation of Salem to follow the principle my dad instilled in me. One of the elders or ministers in the church closes the worship service with the benediction, but I always end my message with something like, "Go back into the world, and live your lives in peace. It may not be easy; you may be up against difficult situations, but just remember: Keep your hand in God's hand and treat people right."

If this exhortation sounds familiar, it should. It's exactly what Jesus taught. When one of the scribes came to Jesus to ask what was the most important commandment, He answered, "The first of all the commandments is: 'Hear, O Israel, the Lord our God, the Lord is one. And you shall love the Lord your God with all your heart, with all your soul, with all your mind, and with all your strength.' This is the first commandment. And the second, like it, is this: 'You shall love your neighbor as yourself.' There is no other commandment greater than these" (Mark 12:29-31).

We have probably all discovered that loving others is not always easy, though. Loving others is a challenge for church leaders just as well as members. People often expect pastors to be more spiritual than lay members, but we all have human frailties. Even when leaders are spiritually mature, their saintliness is more likely to be tested due to their heightened exposure to criticism; you will always find church members who readily disagree with the pastor.

• • •

Unintentional consequences can be seen as blessings in disguise. Being away from home preaching so much had its challenges, but I was always able to return and ease the financial burdens of Salem.

Traveling to preach revivals in different cities and churches also allowed me to glean from the ministry of others, bringing new ministry ideas back to Salem. My vision for the church grew as a result. When I saw innovative ways of doing ministry, I would excitedly bring them to Salem. One such idea was the effective "FRANgelism" program I witnessed while preaching at a church in Detroit.

Traditional evangelism usually involved going door to door, inviting people to church. I was never convinced that this was especially fruitful—many church members didn't feel comfortable doing it, for one reason or another, and many people were a bit suspicious when strangers came knocking at their door.

"FRANgelism" month changed the focus. Instead of going into the community knocking on doors, people were encouraged to reach out to those they personally knew. Each week, members were encouraged to invite someone to church the following Sunday: first a Friend, then a Relative, followed by an Associate, and finally a Neighbor. This proved to be a really fruitful approach.

As I traveled to various churches I observed how being open to change from long-standing church traditions could be advantageous. When I preached for now-Bishop Paul Morton at his church in New Orleans, for example, I was in awe of his shortened ninety-minute worship service.

For as long as I could remember, church had been the focal point of the black race on Sunday. Church was the highlight of the week. It was a time for inspiration, entertainment, and fellowship. As American culture transformed, however, people had more activities available. Leisure time and employment demands increased. They were no longer interested in spending the majority of their time in church on Sunday. I realized that members would feel it was less of an imposition if the service would last only ninety minutes.

In my observations of churches, I learned lessons on what could be profitable and what could be relinquished. I preached in churches where there were very strict dress codes. Women who wore pants were condemned in certain churches. I used to be more conservative about dressing formally at church, but found relaxing the dress code expectations at Salem to be quite positive. Encouraging everyone to come to church in what was comfortable for them opened the church doors to many new members.

Leaders in the church must be reminded that changes come and changes go. Tastes and trends go through cycles, so will the desires of what people choose to wear to church. For years, the deacons and ushers at Salem haven't worn uniforms. On Communion Sunday, they wear white or black, depending on the season, otherwise they just come to church dressed comfortably. I sense a change in the atmosphere, though. It would not surprise me if, before too long, there's a return to uniforms, since they have not been worn for so long.

Because I was traveling so often, there were pastoral responsibilities that I could not fulfill at Salem. I had to be able to delegate responsibilities to others in the congregation. I realized that many had the ability to lead and I gave them the chance to demonstrate their leadership skills. This resulted in a positive impact on the church.

There is no reason to have deacons as leaders if they cannot execute some authority. People will serve when they have a sense of personal investment or ownership of a plan. People want to have purpose in life, and will do well when they feel useful. I think of how Moses eased himself of the burden of handling all the Israelites' conflicts. He appointed leaders under him to handle the lesser issues, with only the more difficult issues being brought to him.

One thing young pastors are not taught is how to handle a power struggle in a church. The more authority a person is given, the more responsibility they have. One of the hallmarks of a good leader is having the wisdom to know when to exercise power and when to restrain its use. Strange as it may sound, power often works best when you don't use it! In fact, once you start to use power, you start to lose it. It is much better for people to embrace your ideas than to make demands on them, even if it sometimes means compromising your beliefs.

Even when you're in a position where you have the power to make a decision on your own, it's often best not to. Involving others in the process invites their participation and inspires their support. There are times when firm leadership is required, certainly, but I have found people are typically much more enthusiastic when I cast a vision and ask people if they would like to join me in pursuing it than in telling them what's going to happen.

It's important to just let go of some things. I might think the ushers should wear white on Communion Sundays, but if the deacon who is responsible for that ministry decides they will wear black, then I am going to let it be. It may not be the best decision, as far as I am concerned, but everything doesn't have to be done just the way I want it. There's no need to be creating a big issue over a question of what color clothes to wear.

•••

As I traveled intensely during the sixties and seventies, I was aware of the change occurring throughout the nation, as well as the state of Georgia. Many people have said that Birmingham, Alabama, was the cradle of the Civil Rights movement. If that is so, its mission control was Atlanta—with Ebenezer Baptist Church and Daddy King and Dr. Martin Luther King Jr. at the helm.

I had followed Dr. King's work for years and admired his activism and advocacy on behalf of black Americans, specifically. I was one of about one thousand pastors from across the country invited to the Fontainebleau Hotel in Miami to hear Dr. King at a conference organized with a grant from General Motors, in 1965. It was at this conference where I first met Rev. Jesse Jackson.

In addition to appreciating Dr. King's leadership, I also owed him a small personal debt. His Morehouse education had been suitable for Daddy to approve my attending school there. Going to Morehouse was the first step I took in breaking free to become my own man.

Though I knew his father more intimately, Dr. King and I did cross paths from time to time. On one occasion he even joked with me about me helping him improve his preaching. That sounds crazy, doesn't it? Here was a famous speaker whose "I Have a Dream" message ranks among the greatest speeches ever given—and he was coming to me for advice? Still, it happened.

"Jasper," he said. "How do you do your voice that way when you preach?" He wanted to know what I did to inject so much emotion in my sermons, how I did that "whoop" I was well known for.

I shrugged his inquiry off. "You know, Doc, you've already got everything you need," I said. "You don't need me to teach you anything!"

"No," he persisted. "I want that tremble in my voice, the way you have it. How do you do that?"

"Well," I answered with a chuckle, "I don't need to teach you anything, but any time you want to come by, I'll be glad to show you how I do it." And we both laughed.

I supported civil rights and promoted what Dr. King worked to achieve in the fight for justice and equality. I was not directly involved, but privately, giving financial support behind the scenes. While I believed in supporting the vision for a better and brighter future, I also felt people needed inspiration and encouragement for living life in any condition, which was where I concentrated my gifting as a preacher.

April 4, 1968, is one of those few dates everyone who was alive remembers—very much like the day President Kennedy was assassinated, or the day terrorists flew planes into New York's Twin Towers and the Pentagon. I learned that Dr. King had been shot dead in Memphis from the television news. I was saddened by the loss, but I was not surprised. We all knew there were evil men lurking to kill this dreamer. Honestly, I was surprised he had not been killed sooner.

Black America was united in grieving the loss of Dr. King. My father was among those who sadly mourned. He had long been an admirer of Dr. King, and had been among the crowd who heard him preach his famous "I've Been to the Mountaintop" message at Mason Temple in Memphis the night before he was gunned down.

Nobody who heard the message at Mason Temple understood quite how prophetic his words were when he said, "Like anybody, I would like to live a long life; longevity has its place. But I'm not concerned about that now. I just want to do God's will. And He's allowed me to go up to the mountain. And I've looked over. And I've seen the Promised Land. I may not get there with you. But I want you to know tonight, that we, as a people, will get to the Promised Land. So I'm happy, tonight. I'm not worried about anything. I'm not fearing any man. Mine eyes have seen the glory of the coming of the Lord."

My father had an unction about the significance of Dr. King's words. He told me later how he had cried all night after hearing Dr. King speak. He sensed that something was going to happen. The next day brought the tragic confirmation: Dr. King had been killed.

Both my father and Uncle Buddy came to Atlanta for the funeral—along with what seemed like half the world's population. Atlanta was congested; every street overflowed with people. Traffic was unbearable. There were long lines of men, women, and children waiting to pay their respect as Dr. King lay in state at Spelman College, the sister school to Morehouse.

Through my Morehouse connections, I was able to arrange with the Spelman security detail to allow Daddy, Uncle Buddy, and me into the chapel through a rear door, to spend some quiet time at Dr. King's side. It was a special moment for all of us, and it especially meant a great deal to my father.

None of us have ever gotten where we are without the help of others. It is important that we pause to honor them and what they have done to make a difference in our lives.

CHAPTER SIX

OUT OF THE WILDERNESS

W HATEVER GOOD I am remembered for, the truth is it's only the result of God's grace. This is not false modesty speaking, but the acknowledgment of what was a privately dark chapter in my life for some years. Although I achieved many successes, including the growth of Salem and the acclaim I received traveling around the country, there was a season when I had secretly failed.

One of the patients at Ridgeview Institute was certainly surprised to see me when I walked through the doors of the well-known addiction treatment center in Atlanta on March 7, 1984. "What are you doing here, Rev. Jasper Williams?" he asked.

"I'm here for the same reason you're here," I told him. I had to be honest: I most assuredly wasn't there for a pastoral visit. A hidden deception, a flaw in my personality, had overtaken me. My willful neglect and self-gratification had broadened into a chasm of destruction. I could no longer ignore what was happening to me: I was addicted to cocaine. I knew if I did not face my addiction immediately, I was more than likely going to die.

Years of hiding the truth from myself and others came to a screeching halt the night before I checked into Ridgeview. My marriage was coming to an end, and I was spending time with another woman with whom I was using cocaine. We were doing drugs and watching the crime movie *Scarface*. There is a scene in the film when Tony Montana, the violent drug lord played by Al Pacino, watches a blimp passing by the window of his Florida mansion. On the side of the blimp is the message, "The World is Yours." As the blimp slowly eased by, I found myself cussing loudly at the world. As if a dam had broken in my eyes, I burst into tears, crying uncontrollably.

Dams don't just break overnight. It takes years for the pressure to build up to a point where the fault line cracks, and that was also true in my situation. How had an anointed boy preacher ended up addicted to cocaine? The same way everyone does—one unassuming compromise at a time.

By the time I had arrived at Morehouse, I was already well past ignoring Daddy's advice about involving myself with too many women. It took a little longer for me to disregard his admonitions about smoking and drinking. I discovered cigarettes as a college student, but didn't consume alcohol until later, and then never over-indulging. Marijuana and finally cocaine would be my downfall.

Despite my father's warnings to me as a young man, I had always enjoyed the entertainment of women. However, I did not feel the urge to get married. My reluctance for marrying may have come from my admiration of Rev. Franklin. He had defied the National Baptist Convention belief that all pastors should be married. I had observed how he continued to have a successful ministry as a single man—and father—after his divorce. I wanted to remain a single pastor, as well. In addition to preaching like him, I wanted to live like him.

I knew there was an expectation for a "Mrs. Williams" when I became pastor of Salem, but people were too polite to say anything directly to me. Once, one of the deacons, who I knew quite well, told me, "Pastor, you need to get yourself a wife... but you need to take your time and pick the right one." I heeded his advice, and took my time.

I got married in June 1971, when I had been pastoring Salem for almost eight years. Although I had dated other women throughout the years, my bride was a lady I met before I became pastor of Salem. With my father officiating the ceremony, we were married in Memphis, Tennessee. Earlier that day, my father had graduated from Memphis Theological Seminary.

I had a marriage of joy and sorrow. One of the joys of our marriage was our two sons, Jasper W. Williams III and Joseph Williams. I am extremely proud of them. They have both followed me into ministry. To see the call to preach flow into the fourth generation of my family is a blessing for which I am eternally grateful.

The sorrow experienced in my marriage was the realization that it was not a reflection of God's intention for my life. Although I was the one to initiate the divorce, I'm not absolving myself of responsibility in our failed marriage. I am never going to discuss publicly all of the issues that led to the dissolution of the marriage; some matters of the heart will be kept between God, my former wife, and me. I will always be appreciative of and honor her for being the mother of my children.

While I did not have the best marriage, I put every effort into making sure we had the best divorce. As time passed, we were able to work well together to raise our boys. We never spoke ill of one another and even, to some extent, became friends.

When I moved out of the home, I took only my books and my clothes. I provided a house, two cars, and a generous settlement for my family that included private schools for our sons. I didn't want them or my ex-wife to lack anything, materially.

As a result of our divorce, I asked my wife not to return to Salem. I knew her presence at church would cause chaos among members. I was determined to not speak negatively. I didn't talk to anyone in the church about our breakup. When it became public knowledge, there were understandably some members who were quite upset. If she had continued to be a part of the congregation, her appearance would have become a total distraction.

It is not surprising that my addiction came during this crisis in my life. But to say that my addiction initiated the breaking down of my marriage is untrue. The truth is that, as our divorce loomed, the drugs became a sharp plunge on a slippery slope I had already been riding.

• • •

As happens for most people, my addiction developed gradually. Some people become addicted on their first drink or toke, but typically it takes time for the talons of temptation to secure a stronghold. That's what is so deadly about cocaine; it creeps up on you like a surreptitious flow. You don't notice the water is rising until suddenly you find it hard to keep your head above the waves.

Was there no one around to warn of the dangers? If someone was aware of how I was destroying my life, my distant relationship with them would not allow for them to offer a word of caution. For me, church leadership was often lonely. I was away from Salem preaching at other churches so much there was hardly an opportunity to develop relationships. And, like my father, I kept a safe distance from the people I was leading.

The apostle Paul writes in 1 Corinthians 15:33, "Do not be deceived: Evil company corrupts good habits" for an excellent reason. The scripture is painstakingly true! In the absence of someone to discourage me from making poor choices, I filled the void with someone who did not mind them. I became entangled with a woman who liked to smoke marijuana. My affections for this lady motivated me to smoke marijuana with her. In a matter of time, I found myself liking it too.

Now, I am definitely not placing accusation for my indiscretion on this lady. I knew exactly what I was doing. I knew it was regrettably wrong. I also knew from years of pastoring, trying to help others with addictions, that everyone tangled up in this web of deception thought it would never happen to them. But, like many others, I managed to convince myself that everything was okay, even as my life was slowly diminishing.

I assured myself that I wasn't actually hurting anyone else. I told myself that I was genuinely working hard to keep Salem afloat and that I deserved the extracurricular rewards and relaxation. I told myself that God understood and would forgive me. I deceived myself with an abundance of lies.

It seemed as though I had gotten away with this deception for a long time. I continued to travel widely, preaching and still making an enormous impact. My financial support for Salem was ongoing, as the church expanded.

You might be able to keep sin a secret for a good while, but you can't hide its consequences indefinitely, no matter how hard you try. As time went on, people began to get a sense that something wasn't quite right at Salem, even if they did not know exactly what was going on. Attendance had started to fall noticeably.

Still, no one ever spoke directly to me about what was happening to the church. This silence became a pretext for persuading myself that everything was okay. If I had been honest, however, I would have acknowledged that the main reason for the silence was that my posture in the church was beyond challenging. I had wrested authority from the deacons, and I was keeping the church solvent with the money I brought back from preaching in other churches. In reality, there was no one in position to question my actions.

My pretense allowed me to think that everything was fine. I started wearing a preacher's robe in an attempt to disguise the significant weight loss resulting from my growing cocaine habit. The hunger for the drug, for the high you got with a hit, had replaced the hunger for food. I foolishly thought that no one would notice the difference.

Once you have rejected numerous warning signs, you become numb to the risk that you are taking. When I first started using drugs, I limited my consumption to earlier in the week. I wanted my eyes to be clear and my mind to be focused when I preached on Sunday. As time went by, my resolve lessened. My intention of not using drugs as Sunday drew near became Saturday being another day of drug binging. Before long, not only was I freebasing daily, I was freebasing multiple times a day.

I falsely believed I was preparing for my sermons as diligently as ever, but in my heart I knew I wasn't. I was putting less effort into the messages. Many times I recycled old sermons that had been received well. In this way, I didn't have to apply myself, and I hoped that the anointing that was on the sermon the first time I preached it would be there when I preached it again.

To do what is considered immoral is bad enough, such as when I went against my father's admonitions about living a clean life; but to do what is illegal—as I did when I was scoring banned drugs—is a totally different level of wrongdoing.

When a person is doing what they know they should not be doing, it becomes mentally exhausting and depleting. It is no wonder the apostle Paul despaired, "I do not understand what I do. For what I want to do I do not do, but what I hate I do... it is no longer I myself who do it, but it is sin living in me. For I know that good itself does not dwell in me, that is, in my sinful nature. For I have the desire to do what is good, but I cannot carry it out. For I do not do the good I want to do, but the evil I do not want to do—this I keep on doing" (Rom. 7:15-19 NIV).

There is a word which describes the practice of claiming to have moral standards or beliefs to which one's own behavior does not conform: hypocrisy, plain and simple. And I was surely preaching from the pulpit the importance of living a godly life while personally living a life of low moral standards. This deceitfulness—to others and myself—reached its peak a few weeks before my *Scarface* meltdown.

I was in my office at Salem when a member of the congregation and her son came to see me. She asked me to talk "straight" to him. Tearfully, she explained how her son was running with a bad group of young people, using drugs and getting into trouble.

"Tell the pastor what you're doing," she instructed her son.

"I'm smoking the pipe," he admitted to me, looking guilty.

I don't remember what I said to the young man. I imagine I tried to look concerned, serious, and thoughtful as I offered some words of warning and fruitless counsel. I know I felt the weight of her desperation, looking to me for an answer for her son's dilemma. Little did she know I was secretly wishing to end the meeting as soon as possible so I could slip into the shower of my apartment in the rear of my office to pick up my own pipe hidden there, and take a hit of cocaine

As dreadful as this darkness felt, the increasing awareness of losing my anointing for preaching made life more miserable. In His grace and goodness, God used me to preach salvation to lost souls, yet my preaching had become less powerful. I had been weakened by the addiction. Where I once felt full, futility had overtaken me.

There is a saying in the recovery process that "you can only hope to start getting better when you are sick and tired of being sick and tired." Albeit indisputably true, for me, I also had to get sick of myself—sick of faking my way through another sermon, sick of living a lie, and sick of lying to live. It is very gut-wrenching to look yourself in the mirror and see a hollow person looking back at you. The weight of my fraudulent ways was becoming unbearable.

This weight and tremendous emptiness, made all the worse by an awareness that my addiction was endangering my life, had to come to a halt. The Lord allowed me to remember, for a split second, who I really was. It was then that I made a conscious decision that my life was not going to end this way. If God would only give me another chance, I would transform my life in a manner I believed He had ordained for me from the foundation of the world.

•••

I HAD TOYED with the thought of seeking help for my addiction several times before my *Scarface* epiphany. I considered going to a city where I wasn't well known—a facility maybe in Detroit or Phoenix. This sense of urgency would rapidly pass, however, and I would again convince myself that my drug use was not that bad. I had my calamity under control, according to my alter ego.

But this time I knew I was at a crossroads. I was in imminent danger. The night before I went to Ridgeview, I had one last cocaine binge. At this point, I didn't care that someone might recognize me, as happened within minutes of my arrival. I needed help, and I could not wait. The risk of being exposed if I sought treatment in the Atlanta area was no longer unsettling for me. I knew that driving to Ridgeview and walking into the admissions office could mean an uncertain future. It did not matter. I was giving up my reckless life.

The twenty-eight days I spent in treatment could appropriately be deemed my "born-again" experience. I learned a lot about God and myself. The first lesson I learned had to do with self-centeredness. I learned that a man should not think more highly of himself than he ought.

From an early age, I had enjoyed a blessed life. Subconsciously, I felt I deserved it. I was talented and believed it was my own doing, not God's grace and gifting, that had afforded me all my success.

How far I had fallen was made clear by my living situation at Ridgeview, where I had to share a small room with a guy who snored loudly, like a buzz saw. The accommodations at Ridgeview were pleasant, but acutely unlike the comfort I relished in my stylish home located in Atlanta's fashionable Colony Square.

Sitting in group meetings was another reality check. Around the room, there were people from all walks of life. Some were successful professionals and business leaders, while others were just plain everyday folk. Many of them inquired how I, the pastor of a church, had ended up in a treatment center. "Yes, I'm a preacher, but I have my faults and my weaknesses just like you," I answered. "I regret what I did, but I can't deny I did it, and that's why I am here; to repent and turn my life around."

Fortunately, I did not experience any major physical problems when I quit using drugs. The difficulties were in my head and in my heart. I had to examine myself by digging deep, admitting that I was vulnerable. That meant dispelling what I had thought for many years, that I was somehow invincible.

I absorbed as much as I could from my personal counseling sessions and the group meetings and activities. I learned from other patients as well as the professionals, notably Bernard. He was my main therapist, a colorful character who had a caring heart but didn't tolerate nonsense. He had been around addicts long enough to detect phoniness from across a crowded room.

"You need to take it one day at a time," he would tell us. "If you don't, you're just going to be back here again," he added. Bernard paid close attention to those he thought weren't earnestly participating in the program. "There's a revolving door out there, you can use it now, but you'll be back later," he would tell them. "I see how you're behaving. I'm telling you, you will be back."

Bernard loved it when individuals became honest with themselves and others in the group. "This is powerful," he would say in a group meeting when someone became transparent. "This is powerful," he would say, "this is powerful! There is healing in the room when we honestly speak from our hearts."

Bernard played a uniquely important role in my sobriety. However, there was one issue where we strongly disagreed with one another. As I revealed to him more intimate details of my personal life, his focus became my relationship with my father. He stated what he believed was the root cause of my drug use. Bernard felt I was under extreme pressure to live up to what Daddy had spoken over my life.

"That's your problem," he exclaimed. "Your daddy is the reason for your drug use. What you sincerely need to do, Jasper, is cuss your daddy right now, and call your daddy a bastard."

"What?" I was shocked.

He repeated what he had said.

"I can't do that," I told him.

"You're not going to totally heal until you do," he replied.

"Well, I'll be sick for the rest of my life," I answered, "because I can't cuss my daddy!"

My refusal to cuss Daddy wasn't because of fierce loyalty, but gut-level honesty. I could easily spin my situation to place the blame for my poor choices on my father, if it were true; but the fact of the matter was I alone was responsible. I was to blame.

Daddy hadn't been perfect, but he had spoken what he believed was God's plan for me, and he had always been encouraging. The words Daddy spoke over my life were a way, not a weight. I had been the one to become prideful. I had been the one to do things my way, simply because I was self-serving. The only person I could point a finger at was myself.

There was another issue Bernard gave me advice on which proved to be advantageous over my own inclinations. As I grew stronger and the end of my four weeks at Ridgeview drew near, I told Bernard I could hardly wait to get back to the pulpit and preach what I had learned while in treatment.

"Now, Jasper, you may want to take a little time to think about what you're saying," he advised. "You may not want to preach this right away."

I was surprised by his response. "What do you mean? You've done so much to help me, and I can use all that I have learned at Ridgeview to help others."

He nodded at my enthusiasm, but said, "Take my word for it. You'll find your testimony is much more powerful further down the road than if you try talking about it immediately."

Though I was excited about the renewed clarity and purpose I discovered during my stay at Ridgeview, I was somewhat reluctant as time drew near for me to return to life outside of the center. How would I cope without the safety and the support of so many like-minded people? Leaving Ridgeview would bring back dark memories and force me to face unwelcome challenges.

For many drug users, relapsing is a part of the process toward their grueling recovery and rehabilitation. I desperately didn't want that to be my experience. I was determined to make it. Bernard encouraged me to believe that I could. He reminded me to concentrate on the days I was in treatment, instead of what would happen once I left the center.

My motivation for staying clear of drugs did not come from Bernard's words of wisdom, but from words spoken in my spirit, from my father. He had died three years before I drove out to Ridgeview, unaware of the struggles I experienced. Somehow I had managed to keep this disappointment from him.

However, his spirit had never left me. I sensed Daddy's voice throughout my time in treatment. I heard Daddy in my head and heart saying, "Why are you here, J.W.? You have no business being here. Didn't I tell you don't drink, don't smoke, and don't have too many women?" The one thing I desired, more than anything, was to become the man that my father had always wanted me to be.

Even though I wanted to tell others about all I had learned at Ridgeview, I heeded the words of wisdom spoken earlier by Bernard. I decided to take his advice and not say anything immediately about my recovery.

After I left Ridgeview, I went back to the pulpit at Salem the following Sunday. It felt so good to be in the place I called home. I could feel the presence of God in my preaching again. The Spirit of God was evident, like in the days before the drugs had left me with that awful emptiness.

Except for my sons' mother, I didn't tell anyone where I was going and what I was doing, when I went into rehab. Some members of the church must have assumed where I could possibly be, though no one ever spoke openly. There was some chatter spreading within the church, which I decided to address.

One Sunday, not long after my return, I finished my sermon and said, "I know a lot of you are wondering where I have been. If you really want to know where I have been, all you have to do is come to my office after service, sit down with me, and I'll tell you." No one ever came, that day nor to this day. I humbly perceived no one coming as a sign of their love and respect for me.

I was not seeking to hide my past drug abuse; it just seemed wiser to wait, as Bernard had recommended. In fact, those that were observant probably sensed what had happened to me from the way my ministry was enhanced after I left treatment. The experiences I had and all that I learned resulted in a renewed ministry.

CHAPTER SEVEN

A NEW SENSE OF MISSION

A
S IT TURNED out, it would be more than thirty years before I spoke publicly for the first time about my battle with addiction, and it was well worth the wait. By God's grace and my daily commitment, relapse has not been a part of my recovery. I haven't turned back since the day I entered Ridgeview.

In the early days, once I left rehab, I found strength and support through regularly attending recovery meetings. Some of us who had been at Ridgeview during the same time stayed in touch. We challenged and encouraged each other to stay strong and stay sober. Over time, I no longer felt the need for ongoing support. The bonds we had forged began to fade, but I never forgot the people I started with in recovery and what I learned from their experiences.

More truer than ever was the remembrance of Bernard. Many years later, I learned that he was in the final stages of a fight with cancer. I went to visit him. I wanted to thank him one more time for all he had meant to me. As sick as Bernard was, he still had words of encouragement for me. "Good, good," he said, "we can have a meeting now."

I didn't avoid publicly speaking about my addiction, the subject just never came up. Then, in April 2018, I was invited to speak at the Issachar Church Growth & Development Conference in Houston, hosted by Dr. Ralph D. West, along with several other experienced pastors. I recorded several short video segments, sharing lessons from my life in church leadership, and agreed to be available to respond to questions.

For me, telling my story required being totally transparent. I recorded the messages in the sanctuary at Salem, speaking from the heart about what I had experienced throughout my ministry.

Only God could have orchestrated the mishap when it was time to play the segment dealing with my addiction. During my presentation at the conference, something went awry with the projector and the tape would not play. I had to boldly step to the microphone and personally share my catastrophe.

I usually show my emotions when preaching, seeking to embody the message I bring, but this was different. I was speaking unrehearsed and from the heart. I choked up with tears as I recounted how low I had fallen, and how God had reached down and pulled me up and out of the muck and mirey clay.

I may not have been as polished as I am when I preach, yet what I said made quite an impact in that room. I believe a well-prepared sermon has the power to change lives, but there is also a time when a message from the heart may have a much greater significance.

I concluded the presentation by saying that if there were any preachers who were having problems similar to mine, who were caught up in the drug world and didn't know what to do, they should call me. I gave out my phone number and said,

"Just call me and tell me, 'I'm a preacher and I need help,' and I'll know what you mean and I will respond."

Those in attendance cheered and applauded when I finished, which was affirming. Many came to me afterward and told me how much they appreciated my transparency, which was encouraging. But it was what happened in the days that followed that was most rewarding. I had several phone calls and messages from people telling me, "I'm a preacher and I need some help." I knew what the coded message meant. Some of the preachers seemed surprised when I returned their call. I counted it a privilege to spend time talking with each of them. I commended them for their courage in facing their problem, and suggested different ways they may begin to find sobriety. I told them that it might all seem extremely dark for them right now, but there was hope. They could learn from me and my experiences.

I trust that by being open about my past, I can change the future for younger preachers and pastors. I pray they will learn from my mistakes and avoid obvious pitfalls in life.

What I call "my wilderness years" lasted for almost a decade. However, not all of those days were dark. My addiction became more serious over time and, as I have said, God continued to use me in spite of my poor choices. But I must honestly admit my ministry and the church suffered during my addiction crisis. Even though I have the blessed assurance that God has forgiven me, I am still remorseful.

I often wonder how much Salem would have thrived, if it had not been for my waywardness. In fact, I have said many times that I have continued full-time in the ministry, into my mid-seventies, because the church is ten years behind in progress and I owe for the lost time.

As a result, I don't want anyone to ever hear my story and think because I wandered for the better part of ten years, they can afford to procrastinate in making a change. If you are hiding an addiction as you are reading this, I want to urge you with everything in my being, to deal with it now, TODAY!

If you don't choose to face your addictions, chances are a day of reckoning will be forced upon you. I am utterly grateful that God gave me the opportunity to turn my life around before a tragedy or scandal made that decision for me.

Yes, I survived ten years, but that is only by God's grace. Drug addiction is deadly! It has claimed the lives of a lot of people who didn't take their problem seriously. Addiction is not just about you and your life, either. Addiction affects the lives of others around you, including the ones you care about most. Especially the ones that care about you!

My addiction had a negative impact on Salem, and my family. My ex-wife and I worked hard to minimize the impact of the divorce on our sons, and I diligently remained in their lives after moving out of the home. Yet, regardless of my involvement, there is no doubt in my mind that growing up in a broken home left scars on my sons.

• • •

I MAY NOT have spoken publicly concerning my battle with addiction on my return to Salem. However, for anyone who was observing what was happening at the church, there was evidence my life had changed significantly.

The obstacles I faced had humbled me in an extraordinarily gentling way. I began to have new empathy for others who struggled in life. I always had a desire to help people; I just never understood how or why they entangled themselves in webs of destruction. My natural abilities and the gift to preach, which made me feel privileged, blinded me from reality. I now had first-hand knowledge of how easy it is to make poor choices. The fact is, there will come a time in all of our lives when we will need someone to "lean on."

Helping those in need has consistently been the mission of Salem Bible Church. As I mentioned earlier, as a young pastor

I emphasized the importance of honoring the elders of the church. Initially, we honored former pastors and leaders at Salem; soon we were looking for ways to recognize and assist all of the elders in the church.

In the mid-seventies, I introduced a department of welfare, to help provide "well-being" for aging church members. Those who had contributed to the church through the years would receive a small sum of money in the middle of the month. We knew that Social Security could not sustain them, so we kindly supplemented their income.

As the church has aged, so have its members. There are more older members in the church now than when we first started this initiative. As a result, supplementing the income of the elders has become a strain on the church, yet we will continue to do so. Giving to those in need indicates the heart of the church.

The welfare program initiated at Salem was an outward response to a puzzlement I had regarding many black churches. I traveled extensively to different churches, also assisting with the National Baptist Convention's annual gathering for many years. I was bewildered by what I called "misguided values."

Tireless energy was given to the need for supporting foreign missions. And, of course, we should be involved in world evangelism. However, what about the mission work in our own cities, communities, and churches, I wondered? Sure, there was a mission field in Africa, I agreed; nevertheless, there was also one in the vicinity of the black church in America.

For Salem, that mission field was Bowen Homes, one of the largest and most underserved family housing projects in Atlanta. Not far from where we met to worship every week, it had become a den of drugs, guns, and broken families. Bowen Homes was the Africa right around the corner from our church.

The community was failing, the parents were failing, and the children, who suffered the most, were failing in school.

Children should not be forced to replicate the cycle of hopelessness experienced by their parents and grandparents. I wanted them to have a better life. The essential step for breaking the repetition of a life of crime and poverty was being properly educated.

In 1989, my aspiration to make a difference in the community compelled me to take action. First, I inquired about the salaries of teachers. Secondly, I went to the elementary school serving the community, A.D. Williams, with a proposition: I would pay the teachers their hourly rate if they would tutor failing students after school.

The organization of the project was a tremendous amount of work. The principal of A.D. Williams sent me to the area superintendent. The area superintendent made the recommendation to the school board. Everyone was astonished that a church would extend itself to support children in the community. The request was ultimately granted. Numerous teachers signed up to participate in the program, resulting in a remarkable improvement, academically.

Encouraged by the success of the program, I envisioned a more ambitious goal. In addition to the progress we had made with the students at school, I wanted to change the culture at home. Mothers of these children needed assistance to conquer their addiction in order to give their children support. I had first-hand knowledge that drugs were emotionally and financially draining. How could mothers struggling with addiction possibly invest in their child's development?

Operating under a federal grant, we utilized an empty property at Bowen Homes for what was known as the "Granny House." This was a safe haven where older women in the community would care for the children of moms in rehab.

For a year or two the program flowed smoothly, which was highly motivating. But then the Granny House was broken into and ransacked. The culprits destroyed the contents and smeared feces on the walls. I couldn't believe my eyes when I saw the deplorable condition of the house. The church had made an effort to provide hope for the community, yet our plan was sabotaged by the very people we were trying to help. I was enraged and heartbroken. On impulse, I discontinued the entire program.

In hindsight, I regret making such a hasty decision. I came to realize my emotions were a response to what the perpetrators had done, rather than the success of the program. I saw that the suppressed anger and frustration in the community superseded their appreciation for the progress that had been made. For the first time, I was able to understand how poverty, oppression, and despair could lead people to make poor decisions.

Nevertheless, our community involvement did not end. Despite the setback, we had witnessed ample success. We were given the opportunity to apply for additional grant money for community-based projects. All in all, we received close to three million dollars in federal grants. We proceeded with the ongoing after-school initiative we had started with church funds.

The government grants were contingent on us creating programs involving neighborhood groups. We were excited to include the community, and hopeful that change would come in our own neighborhoods. In the beginning, our expectations were realized. But later we discovered that some of the employees were misusing the funds. They took advantage of the money remaining in the program's account at the end of the year, indulging in lavish parties and unauthorized trips. Once again, I was disappointed. A wondrous chance to change lives had again been abused.

I refused to partake in the misappropriation of government funds. Again, I terminated the program. We returned almost two million dollars in government funds.

This action created quite a stir; no one had ever been known to return federal funds. A team was sent from the federal offices with regard to my hasty decision to shut things down. I explained what happened, and expressed the gravity of financial integrity in the church.

Here again, I look back and wonder how the community would have prospered if I had simply reorganized the staff, rather than taking such a harsh stance. Trying to do right, in a manner which was right, led me to the decision I made.

•••

As years passed, we realized that in order to broaden the church's impact we would need to widen our scope. Atlanta was flourishing, with a growing population. People were coming to Salem on Baker Road from all of the twenty-six counties in the metropolitan area. Other churches were expanding by adding multiple locations; I felt this would be a great maneuver for Salem too.

The church was in full bloom! I envisioned a campus in each of the six counties surrounding Atlanta. I asked one of our deacons who was in real estate to make some inquiries. He located 163 acres of land on the east side of Atlanta, in Lithonia.

DeKalb County was at the epicenter of Atlanta's growth. Next to Prince George County, outside of Washington, DC, it was the second-best area of economic growth for African Americans in the country. Dating back to the early 1800s, with its name coming from the Greek words for "rock" and "place," I could see Lithonia being the foundation on which Salem's future growth would be built.

We had added a Christian education center to the Baker Road site by this time, but the building had reached capacity. We needed a larger campus for the enormous vision I had. Lithonia turned out to be the answer—although not exactly the way I anticipated.

The owners wanted $5.5 million for the undeveloped land on Hillendale Road. We purchased it in 1996 for less than half the asking price. Originally I envisioned a small village on the property, with housing for people in need, homes for the ministerial staff, and the church sitting on a mound in the middle. I could see people from every direction, coming to the church to worship.

Before we could move forward on turning the dream into reality there was an unexpected detour. Representatives from DeKalb County came to us with a request. There was a hospital nearby without adequate access. They were in urgent need for a road to come through where the church would have been built. The county was bursting in population and the road would expedite the route to the hospital. In some instances, the absence of a road have been literally a matter of life and death.

It's difficult to dispute such a dire need; after all, the purpose of the church is to be a blessing to the community. Adjusting our plans to provide the road access was a mini-sacrifice in comparison to the magnitude of blessings we received in return.

As a result of the road being placed where it is, the value of our land has since soared. We have the potential to do much more in the future than we first envisaged. At the time of writing this book, we are working with a company to develop the land for the benefit of the church and the community. We hope to be able to eliminate the church's building debt—freeing up money and emotional capital for investment in other projects. We want to create opportunities for entrepreneurs to start businesses in the community. My thoughts have lingered on a business incubator center, and a resource center where residents can come for their necessities.

This opportunity afforded through the unexpected increase in the value of our property has been another example of one of the most important lessons I have learned in my many years of ministry—the need to balance focus with flexibility. As pastors and leaders, we must possess a willingness to change.

Yes, you must have a sense of direction, of where God is taking you; still, you must also be open to detours along the way. When you reflect on the essence of life, it is all about change; being willing to adapt and adjust. For leaders, the challenge is to be able to tell the difference between the definition of principle and the definition of practicality.

Agreeing to the county's request caused us to return to the table of decision. We constructed a temporary building on one side of the property for worship services. We held our first service there on Easter Sunday in 1998. Thirty-five years earlier on that exact day I had preached for the first time at Salem, in Summerhill.

It wasn't long before the Lithonia church was filled to capacity. Salem members who lived in the DeKalb area switched campuses when the new church opened. New members from the surrounding counties were eager to join. We began with only one building and had to be creative in using it for all services and youth meetings.

After raising the funds we needed to build a larger church, Salem Bible Church, Lithonia, opened the doors to its new sanctuary in 2003. The Lithonia church location can accommodate almost twice as many worshipers as the Baker Road location.

With both campuses thriving, we began the quest for future fields for ministry. By this time both of my sons had joined me in ministry at Salem. I was indeed very proud. I foresaw each of us taking the lead at separate campuses, and venturing out to a subsequent location in a third county.

Second only to DeKalb County in terms of growth and development for blacks in the Atlanta area was Clayton County, on the south side, so that's where we looked. We found a shopping mall for sale on Jonesboro Road, a site with high visibility from the main traffic lanes and great entry access. We purchased the site for $1.5 million. I hired the previous architects who had designed our Lithonia campus to restructure the complex into a church.

Here again, the vision did not turn out quite the way I planned. But this disappointment resulted in a greater blessing, which was more than I could have imagined or thought.

CHAPTER EIGHT

THE COST OF MAKING A DIFFERENCE

MY PERSPECTIVE ON ministry is fairly simple; when you see a need, do all you can to meet it. I began offering financial assistance to seniors in the church, which in turn made me aware of their housing needs as they got older. Many were not in a position to stay in their homes as their financial and physical resources diminished. They needed an alternative place to live.

As pastor of the church, I felt we should help provide somewhere for our seniors to live. I had some experience working with the government during the Bowen Homes project. I researched getting federal grants to construct senior housing units on a parcel of land we bought near Baker Road. The land was a former school that had been closed for quite a while. We paid $123,000 for the property in 1989.

I was taken aback by the opposition to the plan from neighbors in the area. How could helping elders in their community be a bad thing? Yet the community was in total opposition to senior housing in their neighborhood. The residents came out in large numbers to the public meetings, speaking out against our plans.

I can't pretend that I wasn't frustrated. We were wholeheartedly trying to help those in need and we were facing much resistance. This was one time I refused to get mad and give up, however. Instead, I made a tactical withdrawal, and found another way to advance.

Reverting back to the Salem church campus in Lithonia, I discerned DeKalb County was a divergent and enthusiastic county. The community was welcoming and the local officials were receptive. And so the Alice Williams Towers I and II, named in honor of my mother, opened there in 1999 and 2002. Remembering my mother at the official dedication was a special moment for me. Between the two facilities, 99 one-bedroom apartments are provided for qualifying low-income elders.

With the senior housing in Lithonia successfully completed, I went back to the first site near Baker Road to try again. I'm not exactly sure what made the difference—maybe it was the fact that people heard how well things had gone in Lithonia. However, this time the local community was much more excited about the prospect of low-income housing for seniors. Indeed, when the 111 similar units in the Johnnie B. Moore Towers I and II opened in 2006 and 2010, among the first residents were several arch opponents of our first attempt to build.

While the Lithonia senior housing facility honored my mother, the Baker Road area senior housing facility was opened in honor of a long-time, valued member of Salem. Johnnie had wanted to build a senior citizens facility close to the old Georgia Dome, near the original Salem church. When he died, he left a tidy sum of money to the church in his will. When we dedicated the buildings at Baker Road, I thought to myself, *Well, Johnnie Moore, you are going to get your senior citizens' home at last!*

One of the lessons I have learned from working on the various Salem projects assisting the community is this: if you are going to offer a helping hand, you must also accept the fact that there are those who will bite it. It does not matter how good your intentions are, people will question your motivation. These people are either indisputably evil, or their experiences have caused them to have a lack of trust in others.

Whatever the source of their suspicion may be, as a leader you have to find peace knowing that everyone will not like you, even when you are trying to help. But when you operate in wisdom you avoid or minimize reasons for criticism.

When we developed the low-income housing units, the church was not included in the daily operations. We initially established the Sunshine Brotherhood Community Housing Foundation, which was funded by government grants. The facilities are currently managed by an independent company. In this way we can't be accused of favoritism nor drawn into residents' disputes. All problems and complaints are referred to the management company for resolution.

Some people have questioned our use of government money, over the years. They feel that forging a partnership with secular organizations of any kind demands an immoral compromise. They believe that Christian programs should be distinct and disconnected from the everyday world, so the church can retain the right to be explicit in faith.

My viewpoint concerning this matter is in total contrast. I believe that if we can use something to provide assistance to people in need, let's do it—even if it comes from the devil himself! After all, God can use the enemy to do His work. Proverbs 13:33 says that "the wealth of the sinner is stored up for the righteous." I also think of the book of Job, and how when the sons of God came before Him one day, Satan was with them. He was given permission to inflict suffering on Job's life, yet he never lost trust in God. What Satan meant for bad, God used to bless Job with more than he had before.

Now, I am not saying that the government is the devil, let's be clear! My point is that when the favor of God is on your life, He will use whomever He chooses to bless you. The earth is the Lord's, and everything in it belongs to Him as well.

A few years ago we were funded for a Resource Mothers program through which older women in the church were able to walk alongside pregnant teens to help guide them through their difficulties. It wasn't an explicitly Christian program, but our ladies were able to share their wisdom and witness through their character and their care.

In the same way, we have a weekly feeding program that doesn't have an overt Christian aspect to it. Three times a week we open a food pantry that feeds several hundred people on our two campuses. If anyone asks why we provide these services, we are ecstatic to tell them it's because of the gospel. Regardless, there has never been a requirement for the recipient to attend Salem; God adds to the church as He pleases. We are merely doing what the Bible tells us.

I just don't feel it can ever be right to tell someone in need, "We're not going to help you because you don't attend our church." The unchurched may not know or care about God, but God knows each one of them by name and He will never turn them away. The possibility is always present that the unsaved will hear the gospel preached and give their lives to Christ. Until then, we must minister to them with our words and our deeds.

Sometimes the needs in the community necessitate professional resources or the expertise of others. When I came out of Ridgeview, I had a strong desire to help people who were struggling with addiction. I hesitated to do so, because Bernard had cautioned me not to trumpet my experiences too loudly. One way I could help, I decided, was by directing others to professional resources and centers of expertise.

For several years in the 1980s, our Salem services were broadcast nationwide on BET. I created a twenty-four-hour prayer line for people asking for help. Our team would pray for the callers, facilitating their connection with professional organizations that could accommodate their needs. The call-in prayer ministry became too expensive to keep on the air, yet we continue to direct those in need to professionals who have the resources.

Our annual Back to School Blessings project provides backpacks and other supplies for children returning to school each year. We realize that just giving supplies isn't always enough; it is equally important that children develop social skills. With that in mind, I recruited a retired principal who is a member of Salem to speak to parents about their responsibility in helping ensure that their children are successful in school.

•••

"Graduating" from Ridgeview renewed my commitment to God and Salem. My further heartfelt desire was to inspire and encourage pastors across the country in their ministry.

I had been doing as much informally for years as I traveled and preached in various churches. Many preachers would come to hear me, to learn from my ability to preach energetically in the pulpit. One day, an unexpected door of opportunity was opened for me: I was asked to preside over the late-night services at the National Baptist Convention fall conference. This opportunity was another unintended consequence of my belief in honoring those in leadership by generously giving financially.

When the newly elected president of the convention, Rev. T.J. Jemison, was invited to speak to the Georgia State

Baptist Convention in 1982, I was asked to host the meeting. I was thrilled to do so, and took the opportunity to raise a sizable offering for Rev. Jemison. I wanted him to know that we respected his position as national president of the convention.

He was extremely appreciative of the gesture. On that same night he appointed me chairman of the committee over the late-night portion of the National Baptist Convention. I held the title for twelve years.

These services were not included in the decision-making process at the annual convention, but they were hugely influential. The services conferred an informal endorsement on those who were asked to preach, and offered an unofficial platform for sharing visions and values. Being asked to preach in one of the services was a major validation of your preaching ability.

Being asked to oversee the late-night services was a noteworthy indication of trust and respect. I was both astonished and delighted by Rev. Jemison's invitation to serve as the chairman. As a long-time convention attendee, Daddy had always hoped he might one day be asked to preach at the conference, but that day never came.

Indicative of the important role the National Baptist Convention once held in so many black churches is a childhood memory I have of a visit to Memphis by Dr. J.H. Jackson. He was the longest-serving president of the convention, and widely admired for his oratory. Daddy considered it a great honor to have him in our home for dinner, while he was visiting in the city. My parents had members of the church assist in making preparations a week early for Dr. Jackson's arrival. With all of the detailed preparations one may have thought Jesus would be joining him.

Dr. Jackson wanted Daddy to help develop a farming program to provide food assistance to churches, but it never came to pass. I know that Daddy was flattered to be asked, regardless.

Years later, when Rev. Jemison gave me the chairmanship of the late-night convention, my heart was joyous knowing Daddy would have been well pleased.

As chairman of the late-night committee, I decided it was time to make some adjustments. Rather than continue to have the services at different churches around the convention's host city, I felt that it was more feasible to hold them at the actual convention venue. We lost the more traditional church setting, but we gained a larger attendance, thereby increasing the effect of the services.

Additionally, I redirected the finances collected during these services. Instead of the offering remaining with the host church, all of it went to the convention. While I was chairman of the late-night committee we raised more than a quarter of a million dollars.

At the close of each conference, I would preach the final night, which always had the best attendance. The exposure gained as chairman of the late-night services enabled me to meet new pastors, thereby receiving invitations to preach at more churches. In addition, the chairmanship enabled me to help bring other pastors to greater prominence, by promoting them at a late-night convention service.

Among those I was able to open doors of influence for was Rev. Jerry Black, the former pastor of Greater Paradise Baptist Church in Little Rock, Arkansas. Years later, he moved to the Atlanta area and became pastor of Beulah Missionary Baptist Church in Decatur, Georgia.

After more than a decade of leading the late-night services, I had grown increasingly concerned that the National Baptist Convention had forgotten its purpose. The convention was no longer the voice of authority in the black churches that it once was.

In my mind, I felt mismanagement of money had diminished the power of the convention. It was never clear where and how the money was being spent. When there is no oversight of finances, we will invariably assume that money is being misused and misappropriated. A level of distrust is inevitable. The lack of transparency ran contrary to the way I conducted church business, as I consistently emphasized my father's strong admonition to use God's money well.

My inquiries concerning the effective use of the money received mixed reactions. Some ministers applauded me, but others were offended that I would challenge the status quo. Things came to a head at the National Baptist Convention conference in New York City in 1992. I spent most of the day praying and preparing what I would say when I stood to address the crowd at Madison Square Gardens, for what would be my final service at the convention.

Moving to the platform was very emotional. I delivered most of my resignation address through tears. It felt as though the temperature in the arena had dropped several degrees as some preachers responded in icy silence. Many didn't deem it appropriate for me to openly question the maladministration. Others showed support by making affirmative comments and gestures. After I finished speaking and stepped down to walk out, I was joined in solidarity by other members of the late-night committee.

Constructive criticism has its place, but identifying problems without offering solutions is pointless. So I ran for the presidency of the convention, seeking to restore trust and integrity in the black church.

My boldness in requesting financial accountability cost me, with the disengagement of many friends. There were also preachers who had resented that I was appointed chairman of the late-night services. They thought I was too young and too brash. They were certainly not going to lend me their support. When vicious personalities and politics are allowed room to grow in the church, we lose sight of God's intended purpose.

I lost the presidency to Rev. Henry Lyons. I decided it was time to remove myself from my involvement with the convention. Dr. Lyons asked if I would remain as chairman of the late-night services, but my spirit prompted me to leave. I was still preaching around the country, so I left the national stage to the other pastors.

The changes I had implemented continued to prove fruitful. I was invited back to preach at a recent convention, where I received a thunderous welcome. The late-night services are sustaining the format I introduced, and providing a platform for promoting excellence in preaching and introducing gifted novice preachers, as well as those long-respected.

Meanwhile, there was plenty to keep me occupied at Salem.

• • •

ONE MAJOR AND unexpected challenge came one day in 2005 when my oldest son—Third-um, as family members call him; Jasper Williams III to everyone else—came to me and said he and his wife, Alecia, felt God was calling them to leave Salem to start their own ministry. It was as though the air was suddenly sucked out of the room. I was breathless.

This wasn't the idea I had in mind. Third-um had served with me in ministry for years. He was later joined by his younger brother, Joseph. The three of us were each going to lead our own distinct Salem campus as we extended our range across the greater Atlanta area.

I saw a lot of myself in Third-um. He had come to me when he was nine years old and told me that God had called him to be a preacher; just as I had gone to Daddy when I was a little younger than he.

As unbelievable as it may seem, I actually never wanted him nor Joseph to follow me into the ministry. I had seen and experienced too much of the dark side of life as a pastor. People can be very mean and treat you unkindly, and I wanted to protect my sons from all the hardships endured.

The fact that both of them did become pastors may have had very little to do with what was observed of their father. I believe the passion was much more a result of how their mother raised them to respect me, and never spoke ill of me, even after the divorce. I will forever remain grateful for her reverence toward me in that regard.

When Third-um told me about his youthful calling, like my father had with me, I asked questions to try to gauge the depth of his conviction. When I was assured he was serious, I helped him prepare for his first sermon at Salem. He was a natural, with a remarkable gift for alliterating points of a message so that people remembered what they heard. With grooming and encouragement, he developed his own preaching gift and in time he joined me as assistant pastor. His brother, Joe, was five years his junior. He joined the ministry later, with his own gifting as a preacher and leader, and we became a team.

Although I had not encouraged their pursuit of ministry, I was exceptionally proud that they had chosen to follow in my footsteps. I could see great things in the future for all of us. Of course, Third-um's unexpected announcement that he was leaving the church unquestionably horrified me. I was truly upset. It was at this point I recognized that he had more similarities to me than just preaching.

"Son, I understand you have to do what the Lord wants you to do," I told him. "I had to leave my father one day to go and do what I believed God wanted me to do, even though Daddy wanted me to do something else. But be very sure that is what God is saying to you."

Third-um agreed to pray about the decision. He came back to me sometime later, saying he was sure that he was supposed to go.

"Well, I wish you wouldn't," I admitted, "but you need to do what God is leading you to do."

While I knew in my head that Third-um was forging his own way just as I had done, my heart was hurting. I felt disappointed. I felt dejected. When the members in the church heard what was happening, there was some murmuring about a family fight, as you might expect. To suppress all of the whispering, I was very positive when I announced the transition publicly. I told the congregation that anyone who felt they wanted to go with Third-um to assist with his new ministry could do so with my blessing. And if any of the members left and later decided to come back to Salem, they would be welcomed.

There had never been a dispute between Third-um and me, but I cannot pretend there weren't hurt feelings, on both sides. It took a while, but our relationship has been restored and I am proud of what he and Alecia have done at The Church in Norcross, Georgia. I have been pleased to be invited to preach at their church, and I have also welcomed them back to the pulpit at Salem.

Third-um's departure necessitated a review of my plans for Salem. Sometimes things don't work out the way you hope because the enemy is opposed to them. In such instances, it is important to lean on God and keep going. Sometimes lack of progress can be a sign that there may have been more of you than God in the original vision.

I saw my vision in the idea of having a campus in each of Atlanta's six surrounding counties. I realized that I had been caught up in measuring success by a sense of scale, not including God. As I look back, I am grateful I came to the realization when I did. We could have easily over-extended ourselves financially, unable to meet our obligations when the economy crashed. In spite of my personal displeasure at Third-um's departure, God was there protecting me.

We ended up selling the shopping mall we had purchased for a third Salem location. We made a sizable profit on the transaction, which helped pay down our church mortgage.

Just as it was important for Third-um to set out on his own, I knew it would be equally necessary for Joseph to be seen as his own person, even as he remained in ministry with me. I encouraged him to develop his own individual preaching style, as he assumed more and more leadership responsibilities with Salem.

When the time came for a formal transfer of leadership, I wanted to make sure everyone felt they were part of the process. When they are included, people will approve of what you believe is best for them. So I organized an official ballot in the summer of 2017. I hired a company that manages official elections to come to Salem and set up formal voting booths in the church hall, to oversee the entire voting process.

On the ballot were Joe as senior pastor and myself as pastor emeritus. We each received an approximate ninety-eight percent approval. As the church moves forward, and in years to come, it is my prayer that this vote of confidence will grant both Joe and the congregation a sense of affirmation and confidence to do God's will.

CHAPTER NINE

SOME HARD-EARNED WISDOM

THIRD-UM'S DEPARTURE CUT deep for a while, but it was not the only time I felt wounded by someone in the church. Learning how to deal with criticism, complaints, opposition, betrayal, and disappointment is essential if someone is going to survive in church leadership. If you can't handle being hurt by people, you may doubt your calling for ministry.

I dare not pretend forgiving is easy, but forgiving is always best. I constantly try to remember that by holding a grudge, I in some way keep God from taking care of the situation. Only when I let go will God take the situation in His hands and make things work for my good. It's not worth allowing someone who mistreated you to hinder your blessings from God.

While I absolutely believe God is better at taking care of those who wrong us, I have to admit that my flesh is not always as willing. I have had to habitually turn to God in my lowest moments.

One man who came to Salem in the early years became a trusted friend and assistant. I gave him various responsibilities in the church, only to find out he had gone behind my back and committed an unimaginable act that hurt so bad the pain was indescribable. I had to ask him to leave. On the other hand, I could never deny that he contributed a lot to Salem while he was there. In many circumstances, this is certainly true, that the good in people can turn terribly bad. We may not be able to sustain a relationship with everyone, but we must recognize the positive contributions they may have made.

Years later, this betrayer made contact and asked me to come see him. He was dying of cancer and he wanted to talk to me. We shed many tears as I sat beside him. He did not say out loud that he was sorry for the wrong he had done, nonetheless I knew that was what he was trying to communicate.

Another occurrence, before my sons started in ministry with me, was when I felt the need for someone to assist me in leading the church, especially with my being away preaching so much. I met a minister while traveling who was looking for a new opportunity. I moved him and his family to Atlanta.

The congregation fell in love with this minister. Whenever there was a pastoral need, he was there. He visited members in their homes and in the hospital. Initially, I was overjoyed. He was providing a ministry we seriously needed at Salem. Nevertheless, I began to realize that, within, he was harboring secret ambitions. He was able to ease up close and personal with members in a way time would not permit me to do. He was gently wooing the congregation to show favor towards him.

Because of an unusual set of circumstances—another example of God bringing people into my life at the right time—his deeds were exposed. He desired to take control of the church by not only endearing himself to the members, but also planting suspicion of me by spreading malicious gossip. This minister had been pursuing this deceptive path the majority of the four or five years he had been employed at Salem. When this deceit was revealed to me, I was furious.

I was shocked by his reaction when I arranged a meeting with him. I told him that I knew he was trying to sabotage my pastorate, and I had to dismiss him.

"Well, I don't know how you are going to do that," he said arrogantly. "You know how people around here feel about me."

His response stunned me, but I didn't react in anger. I stood by my decision and gave him a termination date. I made sure we covered his moving expenses back to where he was from, and continued to pay his full salary for several months until he found another job. There was no way I would continue to tolerate him, but neither was I trying to punish him.

The decision I made to keep him on payroll proved to be advantageous. Rumors were being spread within the church that this minister had been treated badly. At the end of a Sunday service, I asked the visitors to leave and for the members to remain for a private conversation with the Salem family.

When I raised the issue of the minister's departure, some members stated they felt I was unfair to "throw him out on the street." It was evident he had persisted in circulating false information in a long-distance campaign. I produced six months' worth of canceled checks he had received to show people how I had supported him and his family, and that was the end of the matter.

Because I always believed it was vitally important to oversee church finances with integrity, I was particularly distressed when I found people were doing otherwise. It grieved me to discover that a retired senior bank vice president, who I had entrusted with specific finances in the church, had written thousands of dollars in personal checks on the church's account.

"Why did you do that to me, to us?" I asked when I sat down with him. He broke down, telling me through tears of the money problems he was having and promising that he had every intention to pay the money back.

I decided not to go to the police; I just couldn't. But there was something about just forgetting what happened that did not seem right to me either. I may have chosen to forgive him, but what about others he may have defrauded too? I went privately to one of the owners of a business where this particular church member was now working full-time. I placed the evidence I had against him—the fraudulent checks—on the table.

"Wow, Pastor Williams," the man said when he saw the checks. "What do you think we ought to do?"

"I can't tell you what to do," I said. "You're going to have to decide for yourself. I just felt the need to let you know, and to show him I did not appreciate what he did to me. Since I've shown you, I am not going to do anything else about it."

I never heard any more about the situation, although I did insisted on making sure that the church member involved was cared for as he grew older.

When people treat you low, you go high —which is also the narrow road, which Jesus said leads to life eternal.

•••

THE CHURCH HAS been depicted in various ways. The Bible talks of the church as the body of Christ. Many people speak of the church as a community or a family. I agree with both viewpoints; however, I view Salem as being more or less like MARTA, Atlanta's public transport system.

The reason I describe Salem as such is because we help people get where they are trying to go. We help our members move in the right direction, through our teaching and a multiplicity of programs. Like MARTA, the church will always move forward. And, needless to say, there will be people getting on and there will be people getting off at different points along the way!

This is an important principle for pastors to embrace. The principle of people getting on and getting off is a reminder that new members are constantly arriving to be a part of the church and old members are leaving. The fact that members will come and go is inevitable. This is nothing that has to be taken personally, and it is certainly not a measure of your value or worth.

In this regard, developing a team approach to ministry is important. The more people involved in leadership decisions and responsibilities, the less likely it is you will make the mistake of viewing the church as "yours." Believing the church belongs to the pastor is a dangerous trap for preachers to fall into. This trap is especially hazardous for pastors who remain at the same church for a long time. Imagine the entanglement of a pastor who has pastored the same church for more than a half century!

This tendency to claim ownership of the church was certainly true for me when I was a young pastor. I not only felt the need to be in charge and in control, I also felt that because I was generating a lot of the money which kept the church going, it was "mine." Yes, I had the distorted assumption that the church belonged to me. I had mothered and fathered Salem for many years. Then, one night, probably as clearly as I have ever heard Him, God whispered to me, "But it's My church."

You will never know the reverberation I experienced in that moment. I was reminded that all of my labor was not about building my own empire, but building the kingdom of God. The success and development of the church and how that reflected on Jasper Williams Jr. was not important. What was important was whether or not the church was a reflection of God. This awakening prompted my being more deliberate and decisive concerning the transference of leadership to Joe.

Recently, I announced my plans to step down as Salem's pastor emeritus. There were uncontrolled tears from members I had served for numerous years; the ushers were walking up and down the aisles with boxes of tissues for the overflow of tears. I certainly preferred the tears to cheers. It is better to leave when people wish you would stay, than to stay when people wish you would leave. I've known churches where preachers have held on firm to the pulpit long past their fruitful time. To the detriment of their own ministry and legacy, they refused to open the door to more vibrant pastors.

Releasing a church you have pastored for years and years is difficult. The preacher and the people have strong relational ties. The self-esteem and worth of a pastor can often be connected to the prosperity of the church. But there is freedom in knowing that your sense of value is no longer a factor in the decisions you make. You can do what you believe God wants you to, free of concerns about the opinions of people.

The life of Moses gives a perfect example of how to lead others. To the best of his ability, Moses made decisions based on what he believed was best for those who were following him. I observed this in my father's life, too. As I have said, he instilled in me the principle, "Keep your hand in God's hand and treat people right."

"Treating people right" doesn't mean that you allow them to do whatever they want. In leadership, you sometimes have to make hard decisions, which can be done graciously and kindly.

At the end of the day the church is a business. Now, that may be the business of ministry, but it still needs to be managed well. I've tried to be a good manager when hiring and firing people. I've learned that it's better to hire new staff on a ninety-day probationary period. In this way, you are given a chance to see if the person hired has the appropriate skills and personality for the position. In life, there are no guarantees.

Terminating employees is never easy, although I have had occasion to let go many people throughout the years, for different reasons. There were times when employees could not fulfill their responsibilities. There were other times when the church had a lack of finances. The aftermath of the financial crash of 2008, when many churches experienced low offerings, caused us to reduce our staff considerably.

In most situations when an employee is terminated there is resentment. In an effort to bring contentment, I offer ongoing financial support. It is not my nature to allow a former employee to leave without having finances. I extend to each one a grace period. I will inform them they are no longer employed at the church, but I will continue to pay them until I feel that I have paid them enough.

After a while, when the time has been extended long enough, I will call the former employee or have a staff member call, and tell them, "This is going to be your last month," or, "You've got two more weeks' pay coming from the church." I've seen how this caring approach reduces hurt feelings time and again. In addition, these actions keep people from speaking negatively about the church.

• • •

IF BETRAYAL IS to be expected in church leadership, then loyalty should be treasured whenever it is found. While I have been disappointed many times through the years, I have also experienced the blessings of true friendships that withstand the pressures of life.

In the worst days of my struggle with addiction, gossip was swirling around the church about what was presumed to be happening. One Sunday I spoke from the heart to the small congregation that remained. I didn't come right out and tell all of what was happening, but I got down on my knees in front of everyone and admitted I had made mistakes and I asked the people for their forgiveness.

A few days later, Eldrin Bell came to the church to visit me. He was an officer with the Atlanta Police Department—he would later go on to be its chief—and had been in the congregation when I sought the people's support.

"I want to ask you about these things, the rumors about you out on the streets," he said plainly. We were walking together in the sanctuary; I stopped and turned to him. "I have used drugs," I admitted. "But I could never sell drugs to nobody, no way. That's the truth."

He nodded and showed his belief in me by coming to church every Sunday. And to this very day, he continues to come. Chief Bell stood by me when it would have been easier, maybe even politically more advisable, to walk away. I count him a true and dear friend.

The same loyalty is true of Rev. Zachary Lee, pastor of Mount Paran Missionary Baptist Church in East St. Louis, Missouri. Rev. Lee and I first met when I was asked to lead the late-night services at the National Baptist Convention. He was a member of the organizing committee, and walked out with me in solidarity with other preachers, when I stepped down and walked away at Madison Square Gardens. Since then, he has taken the place of the late Rev. McKinney as my "preaching partner." We speak regularly to share preaching thoughts and ideas; weekly, if not daily.

As a pastor it can be difficult to form close relationships with lay members of the church, for a variety of reasons. One reason is the jealous spirit shown when members see the minister relating to someone in the congregation. This is the main reason I have never pursued intimate friendships with members of Salem, with one exception: Keith.

Keith and I first met through the Georgia Pool Checker Association in Atlanta, where I have been a member for more than a quarter century. Hardly a weekday goes by when I don't go to the clubhouse. It is an old "shotgun" house just a couple miles from Salem's old Martin Street location. I love going there to play a few rounds of checkers with some of the "old boys," continuing a love for the game I inherited from Uncle Buddy. The checker club is both a place for relaxation and a workout. I get an opportunity to "shoot the breeze" and stay mentally alert.

I also find the game to be a good parable on life—it's simple yet complex at the same time. In life, as in checkers, everything can seem to be going along well when all of a sudden you find yourself in deep trouble because you missed an important move. You must have the skill to size up other players, and think two or three moves in advance; just like you do in a successful business or in ministry.

So Keith and I started as checker partners, but he soon became my closest friend. We shared sacred secrets with each other. I learned over time that my confidences were secure with him. When he was impaired by a stroke and left unable to work, I paid him to be my "armor bearer," taking care of my needs around the apartment, and as I traveled to preach. It was a way I could help care for him without him feeling indebted to me.

Once I was really upset with Keith. He had packed my clothes for a preaching engagement I had in Macon, Georgia. When I arrived and was dressing for church I realized he had not put a tie in my luggage. This may seem minor to many; still, I was angry. I pride myself on my appearance when preaching; it is an important part of my preparation for the pulpit.

I was getting ready to call Keith and voice my disappointment in no uncertain terms, when my host came and said that someone was at the door to see me. It was Keith. He had recognized his mistake, picked out a tie, and driven over a hundred miles to Macon. He too wanted to be sure I was dressed impeccably for preaching. That was the amazement of our friendship.

While I was desperately saddened when Keith died, I was also relieved for him. It meant an end to years of physical suffering. I continue to miss him every single day, and it's been almost a decade since he passed.

As much as I have appreciated those who have been there for me in my times of need, I have equally tried to do the same and more for others. Bishop Eddie Long and I had not had any real contact before scandals hurled him into the glare of the media spotlight in 2010. It's safe to say we were more or less rivals. He pastored the massive New Birth Missionary Baptist Church in Lithonia, just one exit east on I-20 from our Salem location.

I didn't know anything about the allegations of misconduct swirling around him. What I did know was it didn't seem right for the pastors of churches in Atlanta to turn their backs on him. One night I was eating at Paschal's with a group of pastors gathered to lend support to a political campaign. Someone came and told us there were journalists outside who wanted to talk to us about the Eddie Long debacle. None of the preachers around the table were willing to go out and speak to the reporters. They didn't want to be associated with the scandal and possibly taint their image by association. In my heart, I knew someone had to stand with him.

Outside the restaurant, the news media peppered me with questions. What did I know about the allegations? Did I support Bishop Long? How could a Christian stand by him if the allegations were true? I told the journalists that I didn't know anything about the claims that were being made. However, the church was an institution that believed in forgiveness, I said. I urged people to come together to pray for the church and for Bishop Long.

He must have heard what I told the journalists. He soon reached out to me to thank me and ask for advice. I offered some guidance on how to best conduct his church business meetings in the midst of all the upset. One day I gathered several pastor friends and drove to New Birth to pray with Bishop Long, personally. He broke down and cried as we circled around him and prayed.

At that time I did not know whether the allegations of misconduct were true or not. I felt that, regardless of the situation, he was a brother in Christ and a fellow pastor who needed someone to stand with him and remind him that he was not alone. Whatever the truth of what happened, he had not been abandoned by God. Praying for and supporting a fellow pastor was simply the right thing to do. It did not matter what others thought of me.

CHAPTER TEN

YOUNG PREACHERS, BEWARE!

D ESPITE WHAT SOME people say, I don't believe in a "self-made" man or woman. Certainly, tenacity and perseverance are necessary if a person strives to be all they can, but no one ever achieves success alone. We must recognize that there are many who share in our progress, whether through being a part of our learning and growth, or by providing opportunities throughout our lives.

I have attempted to acknowledge my indebtedness to others by telling my story in these pages. I realize there are many who have not been named individually, to whom I am grateful. I trust they know how much they are appreciated. In addition, I want to somehow pay a debt of gratitude forward. For those who have come behind me, I want to share all I can to benefit them on their journey.

Many people have come to me through the years to ask how they can develop the same kind of pulpit style that earned me the nickname, "The Prince of Preachers." I am flattered by this title, though I don't consider myself in the same league as some of the past illustrious preachers I have mentioned beforehand—Rev. Fields, Rev. Franklin, Rev. McKinney, and Daddy.

I know God did gift me with an ability to preach, though, and with God's guidance I have sought to develop and perfect this gift in a way that would please Him. I could never deny that my gift is totally from God: Philippians 2:13 reminds us that "for it is God who works in you both to will and to do for His good pleasure."

I consider honoring God first to be of the utmost importance for anyone called to preach. Personal application through praying, studying, and developing a unique style are important, but preachers must first know deep within their souls that God has appointed and anointed them for this sacred duty. Without God's unction, the best we can produce is man in the flesh, which will never result in a productive life for others.

Having said that, we can't just take our giftedness for granted. We have to apply ourselves to developing and refining it, much as a raw diamond needs to be cut and polished to bring out its greatest beauty. I always applied myself, laboring to be better at preaching. That is in part what took me back to Morehouse to complete my education, after laying it aside for a time in the busyness of the early years at Salem. I finally graduated in 1972—seven years after I would have graduated if I had stayed on my original track. I know that graduating from college also meant a lot to Daddy, who had been so determined to pursue his own education.

After almost seven decades of preaching, I place as much emphasis on preparing my sermon as I have ever done. I have over two thousand messages that I previously preached, filed in my office. It would be easy for me to preach a previous sermon that truly changed the lives of people. Having stood in countless pulpits I could, without a doubt, rely on my speaking experience for a favorable outcome. But I believe when I reach the point of preaching repetitive sermons, it's time for me to step down.

Preaching remains the focus of my week. Even fulfilling the other responsibilities of leading Salem, preaching is my priority. To me, bringing God's Word to His people is the core and lifeline of a church. There are other activities that can easily consume a pastor's time. These activities are secondary, and should flow from the spiritual direction he preaches on Sunday mornings. I believe one reason the church has lost some of its importance and impact in people's lives in recent years is that we have focused too much on secondary "activities" at the expense of what is most important.

A church can have the best-sounding choir, the most inspiring Sunday school, the greatest children's ministry, and collect unsurpassed tithes and offerings, but nothing replaces the power which comes when a preacher brings God's anointed word to His people. The preaching of God's Word to His people is much like a marriage; two become one, and new life is birthed. Similarly, God's seed is planted in the hearts of the congregation, and the people bring forth fruit.

If I have any secrets to share about being a successful preacher, they are these two: preparation and consecration. Preparation can never be hurried. For me, preparation starts on Monday morning. I begin by focusing on the title or topic of the message for the following Sunday. My research assistant helps me gather information which may be helpful. I read Bible commentaries and related articles, and sometimes study contemporary issues that are relevant.

I will spend the next couple of days reading and prayerfully reflecting on this material, before starting to write. I generally begin writing by Wednesday evening or Thursday morning. I choose to compose with a pen in my hand, because it feels as though it helps me absorb the message more than sitting at a computer keyboard. I recognize my outdated method may be a generational preference. I write and rewrite throughout the day on Thursday, Friday, and even Saturday.

After many, many years, I could naturally speak extemporaneously, but I believe that writing what I intend to say forces me to be focused and disciplined. I like to punctuate every word meaningfully. Making my words impactful has become even more important as I have shortened the length of my sermons to accommodate abbreviated services and the reduced attention spans of the congregation.

When my message is completely written, I read and reread it—often twenty or more times each week. By doing so, not only do I memorize what I want to say, but I also feel like I have truly absorbed it. The sermon is now ingrained in my extreme being. When I stand in the pulpit the message comes not only out of my mouth but through my very pores!

Having the message committed to memory also means I don't have to keep referring to my notes, though I will carry a simple two-page guideline with me into the pulpit. Freed from constantly having to look down, I am better able to engage the congregation, looking into their faces and speaking with confidence and authority.

With everything that I have said, I have learned that you can never really tell the influence your words will have on those who hear you preach. You may get an immediate response from people, but what they hear may not reach their hearts. Just as Jesus taught on the parable of the sower and the seed that fell on different kinds of ground, you will always have members who will receive the message and after time, bring forth a lot of fruit. You never know what is going on in a person's heart, which is why it's vitally important to preach the words God has given.

Preparation will not be sufficient without consecration. We should always ask God to penetrate our hearts, thoughts, and words. You have read how I have had my failures during my many years of ministry, but I have never stepped into a pulpit without asking God to be with me and speak through me as I stand to proclaim His Word. Just like Moses, I feel as though I am stepping onto holy ground when I come to the pulpit. Above all, a pastor and preacher needs to protect his own relationship with God, and keep it the source, the bedrock of all he does.

Truth is timeless, but its transmission needs to take into account how people can best receive it—being open to trends and tastes. For example, members now want church services to last less than two hours. While the core content of my preaching has remained the same through the years, some of the packaging has changed to make it more appealing. Though I'm well known for my passion and "whoop," which still remain the hallmark of what might be called the Jasper Williams Jr. style, I have adapted to the changing times.

For a while I successfully titled sermons that were appealing, from songs that were hits on top of the charts, or sayings from popular culture: "I'm Black and I'm Proud," "If Walls Could Talk," "The Thrill is Gone," and "I Fell in Love With a Prostitute." The last sermon title was a message based on the book of Hosea, which I later turned into a play we presented at the Atlanta Civic Center.

I have always believed in being an impeccable dresser in the pulpit, for several reasons. While preaching is a spiritual experience, there is an element of showmanship, too. Being "entertained" is human nature. People want to see how you look, before they hear what you say. I also believe that dressing well shows respect for the people whom you are ministering to. Your appearance can be a proverbial symbol, too—that God wants the best for all of us, and there are no limitations.

For those interested in memorable fashions, a few of my old suits will be on display at The Jasper Williams Museum and Resource Center, along with other artifacts from my years of ministry. This online resource was established in my honor by my younger brother, Dr. Alton R. Williams, and is intended to help equip the next generation of preachers. Visitors can access audio and video recordings of many of my past sermons. My hope is that in making these resources available, I can "pass the torch" to more of those that follow in ministry.

I have had the opportunity to advise and encourage many younger preachers during my years, but no mentoring relationship has been more fulfilling than the one I had with Alton. Daddy believed that Alton would follow him into the ministry just as I had, but it was something Alton dismissed for many years. Instead, he pursued a successful career as an educator.

Things changed when Daddy passed away. Alton came to embrace the idea that his teaching gift was for the church, not the school. Though we had not been especially close growing up because I had moved away to Atlanta when he was still small, we found ourselves connected in a new way through our shared calling. It was my joy to coach him as he prepared himself for ministry, taking over the pulpit at Lane Avenue from my father.

Later, Alton's own distinct preaching gift and love for God would lead him to World Overcomers Outreach Ministries Church in Memphis, where today he is senior pastor of a growing congregation. He credits me with having helped him prepare for his fruitful ministry, but I prefer to see it as another part of Daddy's legacy. My two younger sisters, Nealey Williams and Janice Williams, have also faithfully served God for many years. Nealey was an educator, while Janice joined the ministry at Salem as my administrative assistant. In our own way, we all four have each sought to continue our family heritage.

• • •

Bishop Long's fall cast a dark shadow over the church community. It reminds me that if there is one single piece of advice I would surely give to every young pastor it would be this: guard your Achilles' heel. We all have that special area of weakness that the devil is going to try to exploit to keep us from being all that God intends for us to be.

My father was absolutely right when he warned me against women, drinking, and smoking. Had I listened more closely, I would have saved myself and others a great deal of heartache. But, like most young men, I guess, I thought I knew better; that I was invincible. As time would tell, I stumbled over all three of the temptations Daddy cautioned me about.

Without going into unnecessary detail, I'll be candid enough to admit that women were my greatest area of weakness. Being single and in a position of prominence provided opportunities to make poor choices when it came to women. That's an honest fact. Some women find it intoxicating when they see a preacher in the pulpit. Being married gives you a greater safeguard of protection, although of course it doesn't provide any assurances.

There will be times when trouble will come knocking, waiting on you to open the door. I remember once I found myself in a difficult situation that I did nothing to create or condone. Two women started attending Salem with the intentions of pursuing me. One of them decided that her friend was meant for me. The two ladies did all they could to get my attention.

They came to every meeting I was in: Sunday services, Wednesday Bible studies, every single event. These women began calling and leaving phone messages, saying God had told them the lady in pursuit would be my wife. The messages ranged from faith-filled to out-right flirtatious. Without being discourteous, I tried to be very clear that I was not interested.

I never did anything to encourage the women, but they persisted with tenacity. It got so burdensome that I began recording their messages. I wanted evidence to prove that I was doing nothing to influence their behavior. I finally went to see an attorney to get some legal advice. He advised me to take them to court and get an order to cease and desist.

At this point I knew I needed to make the elders of the church aware of the trouble I was having with these women. I called a meeting to explain what the ladies were doing and the advisement of the attorney. Word had started circulating among the congregation, and some elders had already heard the rumors. After I conveyed the details, the elders, speaking as a group, said, "Pastor, if that's what you need to do to deal with this, then go right ahead. We're standing with you." Their support was the encouragement I needed.

Despite my best efforts to avoid and ignore the pair pursuing me, they would not stop. Eventually, my only recourse was to take them to court for harassment. The ladies failed to show on the day of the hearing, when the judge issued a restraining order against them. Thankfully, I never heard any more from them or about them.

This peculiar episode emphasized for me the importance of discretion in interacting with the opposite sex. In the twenty-first century, with the power of social media, it is very easy for an unguarded conversation to be misrepresented. It is important for pastors to avoid the snares of the devil by steering themselves away from situations that can be misunderstood or misconstrued. For me, that means always making sure there are witnesses when I am engaged in discussions with someone I don't know. I prefer to have a third person in the room, or keep an open door to prevent improprieties. You can never be too careful.

In many ways, young pastors today face more challenges in the area of inappropriate relationships than I did at their age. Society is much more accepting of romances outside of marriage, even when they are still frowned upon in the church culture. The world of technology makes it easier for people to have illicit affairs clandestinely. But there is another side to all this: the likelihood of the wrongdoing being exposed increases because of the digital footprint implanted in cyberspace.

This danger of exposure should be enough to keep pastors from straying—though, sadly, the number of times I see news reports of ministers getting caught in some immorality suggests many ignore the risk.

I wish I had found someone with whom I could have made a lifelong partner. Not because of what it could have saved me from, but for the joy it would have brought into my life. I am aware that, as long as I remain healthy and active as I am right now, it's still a possibility I could meet someone, but I also recognize it is not a probability. Meantime, I am determined to end well, living with integrity and true to God's ways.

I have heard it said my life parallels that of Samson in the Bible. I admit I can't entirely disagree. God told his parents before he was born that Samson would be a leader for his people, set apart from a young age—just as Daddy always said of me. And as a young man, Samson knew God's anointing and power, earning a reputation for his exploits, as did I—though his strength was in his hands, while mine was in my tongue.

Samson's eye for the ladies led him to make poor choices. First he chose a wife outside of the will of God; their marriage did not endure. Then his ultimate fall from grace came when he attempted to appease the wrong woman, revealing the secret of his strength to the seductress Delilah. I've previously written about similar mistakes I made in relationships.

If there is one difference between my story and the story of Samson that brings me joy, it is the fact that Scripture states when Samson woke after Delilah had shaved his head, separating him from the source of his strength, "he did not know that the Lord had departed from him" (Judges 16:20). As I confessed earlier, I knew quite well that the power of my preaching was diminished during my time in the wilderness. The loss I experienced eventually resulted in me changing my life around.

However, Samson's life and story ended in redemption; having asked God for one more opportunity, he was victorious in bringing death to the enemies of God, as he pulled down the Temple of Dagon. I am grateful for the many years of fruitful ministry I have enjoyed since my recovery in 1984. And I hope to make a significant impact for God's kingdom in my last chapter, as well. I hope to build up the kingdom, rather than knock it down, with what may be my most important message ever.

CHAPTER ELEVEN

MY MOST IMPORTANT MESSAGE

I WAS STARTING to think about retirement when, in August 2014, God gave me a new assignment for the final chapter of my life.

With Joe taking the helm as senior pastor at Salem, I was preparing for a transition that would allow me to ease away from responsibilities at the church. It was not my intention to stop preaching God's Word. God called me to preach and He hasn't told me to stop, so I aim to continue as long as I have breath. My call to be a pastor, on the other hand, came from people, and I believe that season is coming to an end.

Like everyone, I was distressed by the live news scenes from Ferguson, Missouri, and other cities across the country, in the days after young Michael Brown was shot dead by a police officer. I understood the anger and the outrage over what happened, but I could not understand how and why the black community had turned to rioting and violence that only further harmed itself.

Then, in the middle of the night, the answer was revealed to me. The church was going to have to do something to change the culture of our community. Surely there was a way the church could take the lead and help make our communities better? I considered rallying America's black pastors in a place similar to Atlanta's Phillips Arena and calling for a collaboration of positive action that could elicit change. Maybe a boycott would draw attention to the need for change in a more productive way than rioting and fighting.

I called Bishop Eddie Long for advice. I knew he had been involved in different national projects engaging community reform. "We need to do something, but I'm not sure exactly what that is," I told him.

Bishop Long said that I needed to speak with Dr. Sam Chand, a consultant and coach in Atlanta, who I learned was widely respected by many senior leaders across a diverse culture of churches. When I met with him, I poured out my heart.

Dr. Chand listened intently, then told me kindly, "Jasper, you're moving too fast."

That statement totally blew the wind out of my sails. I hadn't thought that I was moving anywhere near fast enough. There was chaos out in the streets; something needed to be done!

"Picture yourself on a plane, and you're getting ready to take off from the runway," Dr. Chand said. "But before you can get to the runway, you've got to pull out of the jet-way. Whatever you have in mind, you've got to get out of the jet-way before you can be ready to take off."

He went on, "If you go to the Phillips Arena, you're going to have a tremendous hallelujah time and create a whole lot of enthusiasm, but it's only going to be for a night. People may get excited, but what is going to happen when you give the benediction? You'll have a good offering and it will be the end. Without a plan for what's next, it is all going to be over."

Dr. Chand's caution made a lot of sense. As we talked, he helped me channel my passion into a plan of action that could help bring about real change, not just stir hearts. I unveiled this plan at an invitation-only meeting at Atlanta's exclusive Commerce Club in November 2014.

There were about one hundred people in the room, including many prominent pastors from across the Atlanta area. There were also leaders from the six counties around the city, plus their chiefs of police and superintendents of schools. I gratefully considered their presence, in spite of their busy schedules, as a show of appreciation for what Salem had done through the years to make Atlanta a better city.

We have not sought to draw attention to ourselves, but we have been able to make quite a contribution to the community, one way and another. There has been the Bible teaching and discipleship that has helped our members be active and productive citizens, at work and in their neighborhoods. There have been the programs and ministries we have provided that have assisted countless people in difficult situations and circumstances. And there has been the quiet help and encouragement I have been able to offer some of the city's leading figures through my personal friendships with them. Indeed Andrew Young, a long-time friend who went on to become the US Ambassador to the United Nations, and two-term Mayor of Atlanta, and whose public service I have admired, credits me helping him get his start in public service. He believes my encouragement to my congregation to turn out and vote despite the bad weather played a significant part in his getting elected to Congress from Georgia's fifth district for the first time in 1972.

So, Salem's long investment in Atlanta had earned us some measure of currency, which I sought to spend wisely in my

Commerce Club presentation. I spoke briefly. I told those in attendance that I was sure we all shared a concern about what had happened in Ferguson and other parts of the country. I told them that I was sure we all agreed that something needed to be done. I told them that I did not have the answer for black America—but that I hoped they might help me discover it.

I asked them whether I might visit with each of them personally on a "listening tour" to ask just two questions: What did they perceive to be the three greatest needs of the African American community they served? And what did they think the church should do about it?

Though they were all committed leaders in the community, they each agreed to allow a personal meeting with me. It took a while to organize them. Over the next six months I visited the leaders of each county for a one-on-one conversation, to hear their responses. I went alone, carrying a notebook and a pen. I wanted the leaders to know that I was coming as a learner, looking for answers, rather than someone thinking they already had the answer.

What I heard from the local leaders was fascinating. The leaders I met with spoke about the need for creating greater economic opportunities, and coming together as a community—citizens, government, faith organizations and more. We needed to help our children have higher dreams and aspirations, and equip them with the tools to achieve their dreams.

I saw a common thread from the various interviews, but I didn't want the conclusion of the matter to be based on my judgment alone. Utilizing a member of the church, I was able to engage the Morehouse School of Medicine to conduct a qualitative analysis of my research. The result was not altogether surprising, but it carried more weight, given the fact that it was drawn from the opinions and insights of a group of respected community officials and leaders.

The research concluded that if black America is to be transformed, it has to begin in the home. This is where standards are set. Values should be taught and examples should be modeled in the home. With that in mind, the single institution best suited to assist parents with problems in the home is the church. Attendance has certainly dropped in the years since I was a child. Growing up in the black community, there used to be a surety that you would be in church at least once on Sunday.

There are several reasons for the lack of church attendance in the twenty-first century, not all related to religious beliefs. One reason is the influence of mass media. There was a time when churches were the black community's social center, and main source of entertainment. Today, there are countless ways to be entertained and spend your time without going anywhere near the church house.

Yet, even with the decrease in attendance, African Americans are still more likely to attend church than any other racial group in the country. Without a doubt, churches still have an opportunity to be a positive influence for transforming our communities, if we will only make a commitment.

• • •

If Dr. King were alive today, I fear he would see the dream he once spoke of has turned into a nightmare. Then again, had he lived, he may have been able to better shepherd the Civil Rights Movement into the fullness of all that his efforts made possible.

As it is, Dr. King's assassination meant that he left the hope of our people on the edge of the Promised Land. So far, I believe, no one has stepped up to take on the mantle of Joshua, carrying his Moses approach to leadership into the Promised Land.

Though I supported the Civil Rights Movement behind the scenes, I have to admit that, like many of my peers, I was privately skeptical about the likelihood of its goals being achieved.

I'm grateful to Dr. King and all those who strove with him to tear down the barriers that suppressed black America.

An honest assessment of the half century since his death, however, must acknowledge the fact that we have not achieved all he hoped to attain. Legally we have made advancements, but in many other ways—economically, socially, culturally— we seem to have taken a few strides backwards.

I realize that speaking openly like this will not make me popular with some advocates of the Civil Rights Movement. To question the success of the sacrifices made in the struggle for freedom, even the loss of lives, may seem disrespectful and disloyal. I certainly am not dishonoring those to whom we owe so much.

And yet we can't continue ignoring the reality of our crumbling communities. The benefit of hindsight has made it clear that, in some ways, the success of the Civil Rights Movement also contained seeds that corroded the black community.

The Civil Rights Act of 1964 guaranteed us a place at the table of the once whites-only restaurants. No longer restricted in our choices of how we could spend our money, we exercised that freedom by going uptown to eat and shop with the white folks.

Only, it was a one-way street. We wanted to integrate with whites, but whites didn't want to integrate with us. They didn't come down to eat at our local community restaurants or get their hair cut at our local community salons or take their clothes to our local community cleaners or shop at our local community stores.

Over time, the black economy that had quietly thrived was decimated as we spent our money in the white community. Getting what we were striving for destroyed what we had. Ironically, it was mainly the white community that reaped the economic benefits of integration.

I'm not blaming the white culture for our demise; it was simply a question of supply and demand. It was a reality we failed to consider or envisage as we campaigned for change—a larger-scale example of the unintended consequences I have mentioned before. Our freedom came at a huge cost, though, because the collapse of the black economy has resulted in the collapse of the black family.

Despite our struggles, Atlanta has remained a city where black businesses can prosper. Successful African American entrepreneurs can also be found across the country. I personally know many black business and community leaders who are inspiring examples of success. But overall, the black community is at a disadvantage in comparison to the majority of the population.

We have an enormous number of young black men standing on street corners with no jobs, turning to drugs, crime, and gangs. We have an extraordinary number of black women raising children without a husband. We have a massive number of black-on-black killings in our communities. Indeed, Rev. Franklin's death resulted from his being shot by a group of black men he interrupted breaking into his home. Daddy King's wife, Alberta, had died after being shot by a black man who opened fire during a service at Ebenezer Baptist Church in 1974.

If our problems are solely a result of racism, when you are judged by the color of your skin, why are most black people killed at the hands of another black person? The answer is racism, actually—not overtly but covertly.

What do I mean by the term covertly? Well, slavery may have been abolished, but the spirit of slavery still lingers. White slave owners pitted their slaves against each other as a way of keeping them from uniting in opposition to the slave holders. They set tall blacks against short blacks, light-skinned blacks against dark-skinned blacks. They fostered an atmosphere of suspicion and distrust to keep their slaves from coming together in solidarity.

Whites were the root cause of broken black families, using them as a building block for their economy. They created instability by separating husbands and wives, parents and their children. It was a system of divide and conquer, and its terrible effect can be seen in our culture to this day. Our black community is fractured and divided, when we need so badly to come together.

Today's rage in the black community is the result of long years of injustice. The negativity is an understandable expression of anger, frustration and injustice. But is there a solution? Corporate America can actively participate in helping renew the black community, but let's be realistic: Nobody is going to want to invest in businesses in communities where people are not responsible and refuse to be good stewards.

I am not naive to the truth that prejudice does exist, and I firmly believe that greater opportunities for black people must be provided. I'm not saying folks involved in the Black Lives Matter movement and other activist groups shouldn't pursue change. However, the problems I have mentioned ultimately aren't white people's fault. These problems are ours, the black community's. We place the blame at other people's doors, and leave our doormats dirty. There is work to be done, and we all must work together to get it done.

Yes, hand in hand, white and black, we must transform our communities, and we must begin at home.

• • •

Bringing together again the Atlanta pastors I had invited to the Commerce Club to make my original appeal for help, I presented my findings and recommendations. They all received what I had to share enthusiastically, and agreed to support me as I sought to develop a curriculum that would begin to address the issues we had spotlighted.

I called the initiative AACTS: African American Churches Transforming Society. I wanted the acronym to reflect the book of Acts in the Bible, which tells of how the Holy Spirit empowered the remarkable growth of the early church, and to remind everyone that we surely need God's help today if we are to have a similar kind of impact.

In time, I developed a series called "Parenting God's Way" in which I recounted for members of Salem what the Bible had to say about raising godly children. The curriculum was well received, which encouraged me to offer it for other Atlanta-area churches to experience. They loved the curriculum too, and came back with helpful comments and suggestions that enabled us to further refine it.

At the time of this writing, we are preparing a complete series for a national launch in March 2019. At this time I hope to bring black church leaders from across the country together to introduce and offer this resource. This will also be a time to invite them to be part of reclaiming our black communities. My hope and prayer is that, because of the help of so many who have contributed wisdom and insights, this AACTS initiative will be ready for take-off!

Though I had been anxious to start this program as soon as possible in 2014, I can now see the value of waiting. Beyond merely expressing concern, we now have positive steps to recommend. Many fatal interactions with police have occurred since Michael Brown's death—Erik Garner in New York City and Freddie Gray in Baltimore, among sadly too many others—sparking further angry and destructive reactions. The need for black America to face its dilemma is greater than ever.

The good news is that the solution isn't rocket science, as the saying goes. We just need to get back to basics—decency, respect, and treating others with dignity. Getting our young men to simply pull up their paints would be an enormous milestone! Seriously: we have to stop allowing bad examples set the standards for our youth. Walking with trousers halfway down your butt isn't fashion, it's foolishness.

I know music and styles change. I know people see rap music as a powerful medium for expression of rage and injustice. This may be true, but don't tell me that there's something positive in music and accompanying videos that celebrate drinking and drugs. Rap artists say being a man means swaggering around waving a gun and treating women as bitches and whores. Personally, I feel that rap music may have made some people rich, but it hasn't enriched our culture.

The root of these different societal weeds we need to uproot can be traced back to the breakdown in the home. When young men grow up without a father, they generally lack discipline and self-control. There is no one present to show them what it means to be a man. Black boys are twice as likely as Hispanic boys and three times as likely as white boys to grow up without their biological father in the home.

When women do not have a man in their lives they can rely on, they have to be strong or they will be abused. I have high regard for the many single mothers doing all they can to raise their children alone. Many times these women work two or three jobs and often play the role of both mom and dad. Many have succeeded against the odds, but there must be more if we are to see a broad social impact in our homes and communities.

Unfortunately, some single moms have failed because the load is too heavy a burden to carry alone. It is no wonder women have become hard and bitter. I am glad for the freedom and equality women of all races have achieved during my lifetime, but I also see a lack of discretion, which concerns me. In place of femininity there is a fierceness that may have come from the need to be assertive, because the man has abdicated his responsibility. Furthermore, I see women not only seeking to provide the strength men are withholding by their absence, but also adopting a similar carelessness or negligence, even, in their romantic relationships.

With insecurity and uncertainty at home, is it any wonder that our children are growing up confused and careless in the way they view themselves, relationships, authority and responsibility? Is it any wonder that with no strong sense of family in the home, they look for it elsewhere—on the streets, in gangs? The only way we can hope to raise a stable generation is by giving them a stable foundation on which to stand.

"Parenting God's Way" combines biblical wisdom with practical application. The goal is to help parents better understand their cornerstone role in developing their children's character. It employs practical illustrations, like packets of seeds that need watering and nourishment to flourish, and a box of Bounce fabric softener to remind participants that with God's help they can "bounce back" from even the toughest situations. The sessions guide couples, blended families, and single parents through issues like respect for authority, discipline, and dealing with pressures related to dating and drugs, and social media.

None of this is unfamiliar, but it is undeniably, desperately necessary. Of all the thousands of messages I have preached through the past seven decades, this message—that black America's hope is to be found in black America's home—is probably the most crucial and potentially the most influential. Transforming the home in the black community will be my focal point during my final years of preaching.

CHAPTER TWELVE

HONORING THE 'QUEEN OF SOUL'

INEVER COULD have imagined that I would be given the opportunity to share what I describe as the most important message of my preaching ministry with my largest-ever audience. Yet, I found myself doing exactly that on August 31, 2018. On that day I spoke to thousands of people in a packed sanctuary and millions around the world as they watched the live broadcast of the funeral of the "Queen of Soul," Aretha Franklin.

I was surprised and honored when asked to deliver the eulogy for her father, in 1984. As I have previously mentioned, being perhaps the greatest black preacher of the 20th century, Rev. C.L. Franklin had been largely influential in many pastors' lives, and especially mine. He was second only to my father in importance in shaping and forming who I would become. Preaching his funeral was a special moment I will always remember.

Though our families were intertwined from when our fathers were just starting to preach, in Mississippi, Aretha and I did not really get to know each other until we were grown. She was born at the family's home on Lucy Street in Memphis, on March 25, 1942. By the time I came into the world the following summer, my parents had moved from their home farther down the street from the Franklins to one on Hamilton Street.

Though Daddy and Rev. Franklin knew each other, they were not particularly close. They shared a silent rivalry not uncommon to young men trying to make a name for themselves in any walk of life. Uncle Buddy somehow transcended that caution peers often had of each other, however. He and Rev. Franklin became the best of friends, transferring their competitiveness to the checkerboard, over which they would talk affectionate smack to one another, and also share a deep camaraderie.

We did not have a lot of direct contact with the Franklins after they moved from Memphis, but I followed his ministry growth closely. I wanted very much to be like Rev. Franklin. In some ways, I was secretly pleased when the church that called me to be its pastor turned out to be named Salem Missionary Baptist Church—it was an echo of New Salem Baptist Church, which Rev. Franklin had led when he was in Memphis.

Listening to him on record was like learning a lesson in school. To hear him preach in person was like learning from a master instructor. I had the opportunity to glean from one of his sermons when he came to preach in Atlanta. It was not long after I had become the pastor of Salem. I felt highly esteemed when he sought me out and asked me to accompany him to the auditorium where he was preaching. Rev. Franklin introduced me to everyone before he spoke. He talked about our family connection and the bond we shared.

It was indeed an honor to have him acknowledge me in this way, but I was even more greatly moved to have the opportunity to introduce him to my own church, a few years later. The month after Salem moved to our new home on Baker Road, Rev. Franklin came to the church as our special guest preacher. To have him stand and speak from my pulpit was a very proud and humbling experience.

The first time Aretha and I met in person was one Sunday night after she had participated in one of her father's service broadcasts, while I was visiting Detroit. Because we knew of each other through our shared family history, we began a relationship as though we were old friends who were simply continuing where we had left off the last time we saw each other.

By this time she had already been crowned the "Queen of Soul," and bridged the gap between church and secular music. I say "bridged" rather than crossed over, because although Aretha may have found fame and fortune in the secular world, she never forgot or turned her back on her church roots. In fact, she would return frequently, not only to sing for her father, but to record gospel music. Aretha's 1972 live album, *Amazing Grace*, won her a Grammy for Best Soul Gospel Performance, and would go on to sell more than two million copies, making it the best-selling live gospel release of all time.

This steadfast love of hers for gospel music is how I became not only a friend, but a recording partner, in 1987. When Aretha went to New Bethel Baptist Church in Detroit, her late father's church, to record a live album, I was one of three preachers asked to participate. In addition, there was Rev. Jesse Jackson and Rev. Donald Parsons, who was a popular pastor at Mount Calvary Baptist Church on Chicago's South Side.

The song "Higher Ground" was featured on Aretha's *One Lord, One Faith, One Baptism* live release. On it I got to preach briefly about how, though things might be hard, we had to keep pressing on and looking up to Jesus, with Aretha's singing a counterpoint to my words.

This collaboration further cemented our relationship, and in the years that followed we would talk by phone from time to time, if not regularly. We were both busy with our respective careers, and she had other personal friends in the Christian faith; but when she wanted to talk about something extremely private, she would many times pick up the phone and call me.

Aretha wasn't part of my Salem congregation, but I consider our intense conversations to have been part of my calling as a minister, therefore I will never disclose the details of what we talked about, other than to say that, as a single mother, she shared some intimate family concerns, seeking my counsel and wisdom as a pastor.

While she was a vocal and public supporter of civil rights, she was also a discreet and private supporter of church ministry. Salem was only one of a plethora of churches across the country to which she would give money to help fund their efforts in the community.

I had not heard from Aretha in quite a while when she called one day in 2016. She was scheduled to appear at Atlanta's famous Fox Theater, she told me, and she wanted to know whether I would be amenable to coming onstage and performing "Higher Ground" with her. I told her I'd be delighted.

The much anticipated reunion never took place, because the concert was canceled, but Aretha and I remained in touch. The last time we spoke was a couple of months before she died, when she called again to discuss a family concern.

Though she had always been private about her personal health, despite media speculation for years, I knew she was sick.

"Aretha," I told her, "you still sound well, your voice is good."

"Well, I'm struggling, Jasper," she told me. "As long as I can keep my blood work numbers right, I will be okay. The man upstairs, he takes care of the rest of it."

We talked a while longer, and before we ended the conversation, I assured her that I would keep her and her family in my prayers.

• • •

Although she was too sick to speak to me directly, Aretha had a trusted family member call me five days before she died. Aretha wanted to know, the family member stated, whether I would preach her funeral when she transitioned. I was saddened to realize that her time was imminent, but also touched by her request.

"You tell Aretha that if she wants me to preside, if she wants me to sing, if she wants me to give a few remarks, whatever her wishes are, I will do that," I said.

The family member on the other end of the phone cut me off before I could go on. "Aretha wants you to do the eulogy," they said.

"Well," I said, "then you tell Aretha I will be honored to preach her eulogy, and if I should be the longest of us to live, I will do just that!"

A day or so later, I got a call from Rev. Jesse Jackson. He and Stevie Wonder had visited with Aretha as she faded into eternity, to discuss her funeral. "Jasper," he said with what sounded like a smile in his voice, "you beat me again." Confirming Aretha's wish for me to preach her funeral, he recalled how I had been selected over him to preach her father's eulogy many years earlier. "You have got a better whoop than I have!" he said, and we both laughed.

Only when someone called later that week and told me Aretha had succumbed to pancreatic cancer did the magnitude of what I had been asked to do really begin to hit me. I still half-expected the awesome task would be given to someone more notable, perhaps even President Obama.

But as preparations for a day to honor Aretha, her life, and her music drew near, it became clearer that I had been given this astounding responsibility. And the big question was: How do you honor someone of such renowned stature?

The answer to this question was not something only I pondered; the media around the world wanted to know too. We eventually held a press conference at Salem where I guardedly told a group of journalists about my relationship with Aretha, so as not to betray any confidences. There and even later, when I appeared on a live interview with CNN, I asked people to pray for me as I prepared the message for the "Queen of Soul."

Initially, I considered preparing a message centered on the story from the Bible of the woman with the alabaster jar of oil who used it to anoint Jesus' feet. I felt this passage spoke of how Aretha had used her gift to the glory of God. But as the whole world appeared saddened by her passing, time and time again she was remembered as the "Queen of Soul," and I sensed this was where the Lord was leading me.

The August 31 service at Greater Grace Temple in Detroit came at the end of a week of celebration and commemoration of Aretha's life and artistry. Every television news program, every website, every publication was filled with stories highlighting the impact her music had made on the world. Before the service began, Aretha had been honored and recognized by countless celebrities and stars.

My contribution would not come until the end of a long day of further celebrations and commemorations, broadcast live around the world. From a funeral procession featuring more than one hundred pink Cadillacs—a nod to her 1985 hit single, "Freeway of Love"—to performances by music greats like Chaka Khan, Gladys Knight, Smokey Robinson, and Stevie Wonder, the day was filled with acknowledgments of her musical legacy.

A remarkable array of people stepped up to speak respectfully and affectionately of Aretha; from President Bill Clinton and former US Attorney General Eric Holder to Detroit Mayor Mike Duggan and legendary music producer Clive Davis. Some paid tribute to Aretha's support of the civil rights movement, while others shared personal stories from their relationship with her.

Knowing the day would be long, I spent the first half of the service quietly meditating in the pastor's office. I followed the commemorations on television as I consecrated myself for the task I had been assigned. Later, midway into the service, I eased onto the platform.

By the time I was introduced by Bishop Charles H. Ellis III, who was presiding, the service had been going on for almost seven hours, and was already a couple of hours behind schedule. Many speakers over-extended their carefully allotted time at the podium. Gauging the atmosphere, I knew two things: as much as they wanted to honor Aretha, most of the people in the church were extremely exhausted, and they were not interested in being entertained by more personal anecdotes.

As I stepped to the lectern, I began revising the message I had spent so much time preparing. First, I omitted one of two songs I had planned to sing with Dottie Peoples, choosing to sing, "Father, I Stretch My Hand to Thee." This was an old classic widely known as Rev. Franklin's "prayer hymn" which, I noted, I had also sung at his funeral 34 years previously, almost to the very day.

Introducing the subject of my eulogy, "Aretha, the Queen of Soul," I was conscious of the weariness that the audience must be feeling by now. Although I had one eye on the clock, I knew that hurrying through the message would be a disservice to Aretha's legacy. I was obligated, in honor of her, to share what I felt God had laid on my heart. So, I took the privilege that had been afforded me, and did not rush the message.

Most of the speakers prior to me had recalled their personal relations with Aretha. I excluded a lot of what I had intended to say about our family histories. Instead, I was deliberate in focusing on what I believed truly honoring her as the "Queen of Soul" required of us, which was more important than just saying nice things about her. Honoring Aretha Franklin means working for the betterment of the black community as she had done through her support of the civil rights movement.

Bringing change to our community requires, first and foremost, facing the way things are. This, of course, was the reason I spoke about the problems we need to address; for example, black-on-black crime, too many fatherless homes, and how black America has lost its soul.

"There's got to be a better way," I said. "We must stop this today. Think down, look down, walk down, talk down, act down. Most times, we're low down." Some with good memories may have recognized those words, which echoed what I'd spoken in my "Higher Ground" duet recording with Aretha years earlier.

I also made reference to Aretha's music as I pointed to the way forward in my closing comments. "Aretha, the Queen of Soul, told us all we need to have is a little 'Respect'. I heard her saying, R-E-S-P-E-C-T," I said, echoing the title of her 1967 hit single. "The Queen did what she could," I concluded, "but it's time now for us to do what we can..."

• • •

As I made my way to the rear of the platform, I was greeted by a long-time friend and well-respected pastor who pumped my hand and told me, "That was preaching, Jasper! That was preaching!" He put his hand in his pocket, pulled out a $100 dollar bill and gave it to me as a friendly sign of his approval.

Not everyone in the service appreciated what I said, however. I heard some applause and amens as I was speaking, but I also sensed a bit of resistance in the atmosphere. It was much later when I started to learn of the comments and criticisms swirling on social media from people who didn't like my message.

A few people complained that I didn't talk about Aretha enough. Some criticized me for referring to some of the challenges the Franklin family had faced. Others said I was wrong to talk negatively about the black community. However, many people agreed with what I preached but thought that the funeral was the wrong place to speak the well-known truth. Yet there were a great number of people who welcomed my message.

When I got to Salem the following Sunday, I was greeted by applause and praises and thank-you's from members of the congregation for speaking so boldly. In the days that followed, the church received phone calls and email messages from all over the world, thanking me for the message I had delivered.

The negative comments I received were somewhat harsh, but those comments did not dampen my spirit. When you have been preaching as long as I have, you become used to people disagreeing with what you say. I chose to let it go. Instead, I searched my heart to see whether I'd done what I sensed God had directed me to, and as I looked back I felt that I had honored Aretha to the best of my ability; by calling on the black community to be part of realizing the progress she longed for in her lifetime.

Given the publicity surrounding the criticisms, I decided to hold another press conference at Salem, to give members of the media a chance to ask any questions they might have. "I want to see Aretha's life immortalized," I told them, "and because of the great contributor that she was to the Civil Rights Movement, and the support that she gave, my efforts to turn black America around, would be pleasing to her."

My long-time friend Rev. Dr. Gerald Durley, senior pastor of Providence Missionary Baptist Church, in Atlanta, stood by me as I answered questions, along with faithful Salem member Eldrin Bell. As the press conference concluded, Dr. Durley asked if he might say a few words.

"All throughout time there's always been a prophetic voice that has come forth," he said when he stepped forward to the microphone. "Now, what's interesting about prophecies is that... people might not understand at that moment or even weeks later, but down the road they'll begin to understand how the dots were connected. When we talk about the freedom that Dr. King spoke about in alleviating the pain in our community, that's what I think this man of God has said, and what he has done."

"Was the funeral the right time to raise the issues?" he questioned. "I don't know a right time and a right platform," Dr. Durley said. "When the Spirit of God says speak truth to power and you do it, then it's the right time."

The controversy continued in the days that followed, with a member of the Franklin family saying he had been disappointed in the eulogy. Out of respect for the family and my dear friend Aretha, I chose not to respond.

It was interesting to see the responses as people who had only followed news reports about what I said went and listened to my message for themselves. Typical of the reaction was this man's online comment: "I didn't see this part of the funeral but I saw some of the 'blacklash' and thought he made horrible, unimaginable comments. But when I heard the message in its entirety, I see he was spot on," he wrote. "People take things out of context without grasping the meaning."

Another man commented, "I don't see how anyone could be upset at anything he said. Just about everything he said is the truth about the black community as it stands today; people can't handle the truth! Point of the matter is nobody else at that funeral had the spine to stand up and do what he did! Anytime anyone speaks about empowering our community the status quo will always have a problem with it and try to demonize it! Anyone black against what this man is trying to do is nothing more than a sellout to Massa! He chose the perfect platform to deliver this message!"

After watching a video of my eulogy, one young woman posted, "There is a reason why Miss Aretha wanted this preacher to preach her eulogy. She was very much invested in the uprising of the Black community and the preacher is bringing her messages through himself."

While a large majority of the media was antagonistic to what I said, there were some supportive voices. In an opinion piece in the *Wall Street Journal*, Shelby Steele, a senior fellow at Stanford University's Hoover Institution, noted, as I had, how black-on-black violence did not get much attention.

"White-on-black shootings evoke America's history of racism and so carry an iconic payload of menace," he wrote a month after the funeral. "Black-on-black shootings carry no such payload, although they are truly menacing to the black community. They evoke only despair."

As people continued to debate the positives and negatives of my message, it became clear to me that this was another of those unintended consequence moments in my ministry—perhaps the most important one of all.

It was never my intention to be controversial. I had not tried to use the funeral for personal gain. I simply went to honor a friend in the best way I knew how, by trying to inspire people to show their love and appreciation for a woman who had been a large part of their lives by working to bring about more of the dreams she had hoped for—loving families in a healthy community.

I was encouraged to see that, as a result of what I said, people were talking about hard issues. As a result of my unsought and unexpected moment in the media spotlight, there has been heightened interest in the AACTS initiative. At the time of this writing, we're working on a conference to be held in Atlanta in March of 2019. This conference will bring together leaders across religious and racial lines from all over America and other parts of the world to see how, collectively, we might turn black America around.

We may not all agree on exactly what the answers are; however, we can start to discuss the questions, hear from each other, and see how we might work together in a way that would truly honor the "Queen of Soul."

The disparities, the ills and the ails in our community have thinned the number of her "subjects." Having preached for almost seventy years, and having pastored the same congregation for almost fifty-seven years, I am committing the remainder of my life to helping create more "subjects" for the "Queen of Soul." This is the focus of my final push as a person, a pastor, and a preacher: I commit my last days to being part of restoring black America, to God's glory. Amen!

Further Resources

I hope that you may have found some inspiration and encouragement in reading my story. If so, you might be interested to discover further resources at:

My personal website:
www.jasperwilliams.com
My personal Facebook page:
www.facebook.com/jasperwilliamsjr

The Jasper Williams Museum and Resource Center:
www.jasperwilliams.com/museum

Salem Bible Church:

**2283 Baker Road NW
Atlanta, Georgia 30318**

Email:
info@salembiblechurch.org

Salem Bible Church website:
www.salembinblechurch.org

Salem Bible Church Facebook page:
www.facebook.com/salembibleministries

Salem Bible Church YouTube page:
www.youtube.com/user/sbcjw45

African American Churches Transforming Society (AACTS)
www.aacts.info

CPSIA information can be obtained
at www.ICGtesting.com
Printed in the USA
LVHW040057250119
605101LV00001B/1

9 781943 294923